Praise for *The Journey To Teams...*

I successfully implemented teams at Alcatel before I read this book, but only after four years of dead ends and wrong turns — a result of reading traditional team building books and using traditional team building consultants. This book would have saved us at least two years and lots of headaches. Subsequently, I used The Journey To Teams *as our team implementation road map when I was hired as director of manufacturing at Sumitomo. Within two years we were making record profits, and I was promoted to VP of manufacturing. I recently accepted a new position, and* The Journey To Teams *will be required reading for all my managers.*

  - Roger Clarizio, Director of Operations, Krone, Inc.

Fresh, clear, logical thinking about team implementation. Easily readable by everyone at every level of the organization. I've read it nine times and each time I learned something new. Don't expect any of the traditional team-building stuff that treats teams as the objective. This book treats teams as a means to real objectives - more capable people, producing better business results.

  - Michael Seleway, Project Manager, Teams Implementation, Cape Canaveral Group

For two years I reviewed books about how to implement teams, but everything I read contained the same old traditional ideas that haven't worked for us (i.e. give employees some basic skills training, then ask them to take turns doing various supervisory functions). The Journey To Teams *is a completely different approach. If you want to implement teams, this is the book.*

  - Curt Kufner, Internal Consultant, Fiskars, Inc.

The Journey To Teams

iv

The Journey To Teams

The New Approach To Achieve
Breakthrough Business Performance

Michael D. Regan

with

Mark Slattery

Holden Press

The Journey To Teams
The New Approach To Achieve
Breakthrough Business Performance

By Michael D. Regan
With
Mark Slattery

Published by:
Holden Press
Raleigh, North Carolina
1-888-910-8326

ISBN
0-9663549-5-8

Library of Congress Catalog Card Number
98-93080

Acknowledgements

First I acknowledge Almighty God, without whom I could not breathe, let alone write a book.

Thank you Stacey. You are a wonderful wife and mother, an excellent sounding board, and an endless source of creative ideas. Thanks also to the rest of my family for their support and wisdom, and to my clients and colleagues for their thoughtful input.

About the Authors

Michael D. Regan is the Chairman of Everest Consulting Group, Inc. and is also author of *The Kaizen Revolution.* His company's better-known clients include GlaxoWellcome, Alcatel, Nortel, Borg-Warner Automotive, Sumitomo Electric, BB&T Bank, Mallinckrodt Pharmaceutical, and Cape Canaveral Group. He holds a MBA from the University of Rochester.

Mark Slattery, CEO of Everest Consulting Group, has spent 22 years helping organizations build teams and improve productivity. His clients have ranged from the Fortune 500 to small privately held companies, and have included manufacturers, banks, government agencies, health care organizations, utilities, and telecommunications firms. Mark was a contributor to the book *The Kaizen Revolution,* is a graduate of Merrimack College, and plays a mean guitar.

TABLE OF CONTENTS

Note From the Author

One can resist the invasion of armies, but not an idea whose time has come.

- Victor Hugo

Eighty-six percent of the employees in the average organization are individual contributors. They determine the quality, cost, and delivery performance of your product or service because they do the work. They are very talented – at least outside of work. They own homes, raise children, and hold leadership positions in their communities. Yet when they come to work, most "leave their brains at the door." Here are two interesting and complimentary facts:

1. If your individual contributors used their talents at work, you would rapidly improve the quality, cost, and delivery performance of your product or service, and your profits would increase dramatically.

2. Your individual contributors *want* to use their talents to help your organization improve quality, cost and delivery performance. *Most of them want that challenge more than they want a bigger paycheck.*

You probably feel you have great employees in your organization, but chances are you do not feel you are getting greatness from them. Why? Because we have inherited a method of leadership that discourages individual contributors from using their talents at work.

What is wrong with how we currently lead? What should we be doing differently? This book will show you.

As Victor Hugo would say, this is an idea whose time has come.

Michael D. Regan
Raleigh, NC
July 2000

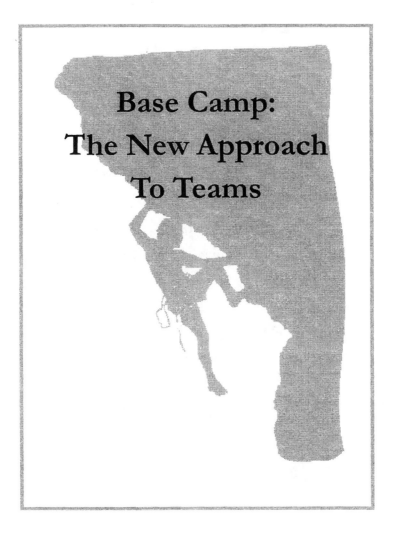

Base Camp:
The New Approach
To Teams

Somehow we have to get past the idea that all we have to do is join hands in a circle and sing Kum Bah Yah *and say, "We're moving to teams." It's just not that easy, and anyone who has ever tried it knows it.*

\-   Michael Shrage, author of *No More Teams*

The Proven Path To Teams

"It would be easier to climb Mount Everest than for us to implement effective teams."

I gave Kevin a polite laugh and wondered what he was talking about. He was one of several managers I was interviewing as part of a consulting project. He wasn't volunteering any further explanation.

"What do you mean?" I asked.

"It would be easier for us to get a group of people to the top of Mount Everest than it would be to implement teams that really work," he replied. "That's how hard it will be."

3

I looked at my watch. I was already late for my next meeting.

"That's an interesting thought," I said. "Can we talk about this later?"

"There's nothing more to say about it," he said. "It's just a fact."

I let it go at that and headed to my next interview. Later that night I remembered Kevin's words. Implementing teams is difficult, but harder than climbing Mount Everest? No chance. I went to sleep and tried to forget about it.

I awoke the next morning and I couldn't stand it any longer. An hour later I was in the library looking for evidence. The perils of climbing Mount Everest soon became obvious. The most dangerous include:

- **The Kumbu Icefall.** Located at the beginning of the climb, this is a stretch of hotel-sized ice cubes, piled precariously on top of one another. It takes the average climber eight hours to pass through them. During the day, the ice masses are constantly shifting as the sun heats them. If they shift while you are in the wrong spot, your hike is over.

- **The Avalanches**. Avalanches and falling rocks are the number one cause of death on Everest. They come by surprise and show no mercy.

- **The Storms**. If a sudden blizzard materializes, there is no chance of moving up or down the mountain. No choice exists but to huddle together on the open mountainside and hope it blows over while you are still conscious.

- **The Wind**. On many days, the wind is so strong that snow and ice are blown off the top of the mountain like the tail of a comet, visible from miles away. There are no handrails on this hike, just vertical walls to scale and narrow, slippery trails to climb. If you lose your grip, the wind will escort you to the bottom of the mountain in a hurry.

- **Oxygen Deprivation**. As a climber moves up the mountain into thinner atmosphere, the amount of oxygen in the atmosphere decreases. Said one experienced guide, "It is like trying to run on a treadmill, while breathing through a straw." Not only are these conditions utterly exhausting, but the lack of oxygen also causes a state called hypoxia, in which one simply cannot think sensibly. Climbers have been known to wander off the side of the mountain, remove articles of clothing for no apparent reason, or leave vital equipment behind.

So much for descriptions. Now I needed numbers. I looked in a few more books and learned that, by the end of 1996, 391 expeditions had attempted to reach the summit. Given the dangers listed above, how many of those expeditions do you think made it to the top?

Like me, you probably guessed a low number, something like 10 or 20. Would you believe that 168, or 43 percent, of the 391 expeditions succeeded? Climbing Mount Everest is extremely dangerous, but almost half of all attempts succeed.

Now I needed some statistics about teams. I looked for a long time and I finally found an article titled "Why Teams Fail" in the February 1996 edition of *USA Today*. Near the end of the article I found the results of a survey claiming that 87 percent of teams failed to meet expectations. Only 13 percent succeeded. Wow! I could hardly believe it.

Kevin was right. It is easier to climb Mount Everest than to implement effective teams.

In June 1953, Sir Edmund Hillary became famous as the first person to reach the top of Mount Everest. People had been trying to climb the mountain for over a hundred years, and no one had succeeded. Yet after he succeeded, many expeditions made it to the summit. Why?

Certainly it helped to know it could be done, but there was another reason. Sir Edmund Hillary had established a path that worked. He told other climbers the route he took, how to get around the toughest obstacles and where to camp. The expeditions after him followed the same path.

If you have tried teams but did not improve quality by at least 90 percent, productivity (blue and white collar) by at least 30 percent, lead time by at least 75 percent and morale by 100 percent, you did not do it right. You got lost somewhere.

Just as there is a path for climbing Mount Everest that maximizes an expedition's chance for success, so also there is a proven path for implementing teams that will get you the results you want. This book will show you that path.

You are about to join a supervisor named Jack Mabrey on his Journey To Teams. He was promoted into management two years ago and has been trying to implement teams, with no success, ever since. He is a fictional character, but I'll bet you will be able to relate to his frustrations.

You and Jack will learn about The Journey To Teams together. As he implements the ideas contained within, his department will perform better, his people will become happier, he will work fewer hours and he will worry less. It will happen for you too. Just keep reading.

The Map

Jack Mabrey had just finished listening to his messages and felt like he was about to explode. Dan, one of his employees, had called in sick again, and tonight was the busiest night of the week. Now he had to figure out how to get Dan's work done.

Jack walked out to Dan's desk and saw the pile of papers to be processed. He continued down the hall and saw Lisa leaning back in a chair with her feet on a desk, talking on the phone and laughing. He sat on the desk in front of her, crossed his arms across his chest and waited.

Lisa looked at him and shrugged. "We've got nothing to do, Jack. We can't do anything until Dan gives us the paperwork."

Jack had a sudden urge to scream. Instead he tried to speak calmly. "Before this job, you did Dan's job. Did you look on his desk to see if there was anything that you could work on?"

Lisa frowned. "Well, I mean, a lot of things have changed over there, and anyway that's not my job anymore," she stammered.

"It is tonight," he said abruptly. He walked her over to Dan's desk and gave her specific instructions about what needed to be done.

Jack headed back to his office, asking himself why he ever accepted this job in the first place. For 10 long years he had learned the ropes of this organization in a staff job. He had finally been chosen for a supervisory job. At last, a chance to be a leader, to do things right, to fix problems, slash bureaucracy and start his climb up the corporate ladder. That had been his plan anyway.

Now, two years later, he felt more like a firefighter or a babysitter than a leader. Whenever there was a problem or anything unusual beyond the simplest job responsibility, his subordinates couldn't (or wouldn't) make a decision without dragging him into it. Then they waited for him to tell them exactly what to do and how to do it. They rarely put forth any extra effort on the job, and it was a constant challenge just to get them to do the minimum.

The worst part was that he knew it was his own fault. He was not the leader his people needed. He didn't know how to inspire them or how to make work challenging and interesting for them.

The ring of the telephone interrupted his thoughts, and he suddenly remembered that he and his wife had an out-of-town guest arriving tonight. Jack looked quickly at his watch and his stomach turned. It was 6:25 p.m. His company was expected to arrive at 6:30 p.m. He picked up the phone and answered weakly, "Hello?"

He was in big trouble.

Forty-five minutes later he pulled into the driveway. Jack could see his wife and their long-time friend, Jangbu*, sitting on the front porch. Jack was anxious to see him again. He slid his car into the garage and went inside to clean up.

As he washed, he thought about his Uncle Jangbu. It had been a few years since they had seen each other.

---

* Pronounced *JUNG-BOO*

11

Jangbu was not really his uncle, but Jack certainly thought of him that way. Jangbu Makti had guided Jack's father to the top of Mount Everest 27 years ago, and the two had remained close friends until his father's death six months ago.

Since their meeting, Jangbu had visited with Jack's parents every few years at the end of the climbing season. Jack always loved listening to the stories of Mount Everest and how Jangbu worked as a Sherpa guide for expeditions up the world's tallest mountain.

Jack opened the screen door and walked onto the porch. "Uncle Jangbu," he said.

"Ah, Jack," Jangbu said, embracing him warmly. "It is good to see you again. I have missed you." Jangbu spoke English fairly well, having worked with westerners on the mountain six months of every year. Still, Jack had to listen carefully to understand his accent.

"I've missed you too, Uncle Jangbu," said Jack as they shook hands. "Sorry I'm late."

"You'd better be," his wife Nancy said half jokingly. "We've been having a very nice conversation. And you're already a glass of wine behind us."

"Does this mean I'm forgiven?" Jack replied.

"As far as you know," she said as she pinched his arm. Jack sat down in the chair next to hers.

Jangbu spent the next hour telling Jack and Nancy

that although he still enjoyed the mountain, he was bored and in need of new challenges. Finally, Jangbu asked Jack about his job and what he did at work.

"I'm a supervisor," Jack replied, "but maybe not for long. It's not as rewarding as I had hoped it would be. I'm thinking of going back to my old staff job."

Jangbu smiled. "What is the problem, Jack? Maybe I can help."

Jack paused. He couldn't imagine how a Mount Everest guide could help him solve his problems at work. What did mountain climbing have to do with business? What the heck, Jack thought, let's give it a try.

"I feel like I'm responsible for solving all the problems and making all the decisions in my department," Jack explained. "My people can follow the instructions in our standard operating procedures, but the minute they run into anything out of the ordinary everything stops. Then they either call me to find out what to do, or they ignore the problem and wait for me to point it out to them."

"Jack, your department is like an expedition that is stuck at base camp," Jangbu explained. "They are like hikers who are fine as long as they have a map and the path is straight and smooth. You want to lead them up the mountain, but they don't have basic climbing skills. They do not know how to blaze their own trail. You

13

must teach them how to think for themselves, first as individuals and then as a team."

"That makes a lot of sense," agreed Jack. "That is probably why my company is losing money. Years ago our quality, productivity and responsiveness were the best in the industry, but now our competition is as good or better. In order to make a profit we need to find new and better ways to do everything we do. There is no standard operating procedure for how to do that. As you said, we need to blaze new trails, and I can't do it all myself."

"We Sherpas have a saying," Uncle Jangbu said. "A guide who helps too much rarely gets his climbers to the top of the mountain. You have been helping your people too much. They must learn to rely on themselves and each other, not on you. You must coach them instead of carrying them. I would like to show you some things I have learned through the years climbing my mountain. Perhaps it will help you climb yours."

Jack nodded slowly. Jangbu's words already had him thinking. "Let's do it," he said.

"I will need a piece of paper and a pen," Jangbu said.

"Wait a minute," Nancy interrupted. "Aren't you two hungry? I know I am."

"Okay, okay," Jack agreed. "We'll wait until after dinner."

14

After clearing the dinner table, Jack found a large piece of paper and a pen and watched as Jangbu sketched a map.

"That doesn't look much like Mount Everest," Jack commented.

Jangbu looked up. "It is not a map of the mountain itself, but it is a map of the psychological journey climbers must make as a group if they hope to reach the summit."

Jangbu drew for a moment more, labeled several parts of the map and put the pen down. Then he looked at Jack.

Jack looked at the map (see map 1). "Well, aren't you going to finish it?" he asked.

"One step at a time, Jack," Jangbu replied. "This will become a picture of what we have learned as Sherpa guides over the last 200 years of climbing in the Himalayas. It shows how we transform a group of inexperienced strangers into a team that is capable of reaching the top of the world. It applies to any group of people who desire to accomplish a goal together. We will have to modify the terms and concepts on my map to fit your work environment. For instance, I substituted the

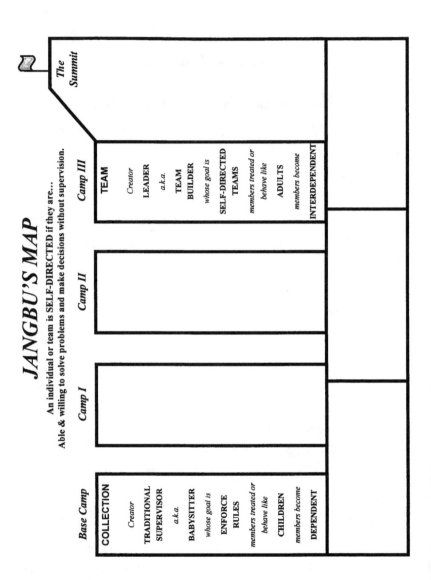

JANGBU'S MAP

An individual or team is SELF-DIRECTED if they are...
Able & willing to solve problems and make decisions without supervision.

Base Camp	Camp I	Camp II	Camp III	The Summit
COLLECTION			**TEAM**	
Creator			*Creator*	
TRADITIONAL SUPERVISOR			**LEADER**	
a.k.a.			*a.k.a.*	
BABYSITTER			**TEAM BUILDER**	
whose goal is			*whose goal is*	
ENFORCE RULES			**SELF-DIRECTED TEAMS**	
members treated or behave like			*members treated or behave like*	
CHILDREN			**ADULTS**	
members become			*members become*	
DEPENDENT			**INTERDEPENDENT**	

MAP 1

term 'supervisor' for 'guide.' You will have to help me express these concepts in ways that fit your business world."

"Go on," urged Jack.

Jangbu nodded. "You see, there are four different ways to organize people to work together," he explained. "Most groups start out as what we call a COLLECTION*. Our goal as Sherpas is to turn them into a TEAM. That is your goal also."

Jack studied the map. "I can certainly relate to the area on the diagram labeled COLLECTION," he said. "My job title is SUPERVISOR, but as much as I want to be a LEADER, I can't figure out how to stop acting like a BABYSITTER, spending most of my time ENFORCING RULES. Although the people who work for me are far from being CHILDREN in terms of their ages, they often behave that way at work. I can't understand why the same people who solve difficult problems and make tough decisions in their personal lives seem to leave their brains at the door when they come to work. As capable, creative and intelligent as they are, they somehow have become conditioned to be

---

* The terms 'collection' and 'work group' (see chapter 2) were adapted from *Coaching and Team Leadership Skills for Managers and Supervisors*, published by SkillPath Seminars.

DEPENDENT* on me to solve all of the problems and make all of the decisions at work."

"It is no surprise you are not enjoying your work," said Jangbu. "If a group of climbers acted that way, I would give them their money back and send them home."

Now Jack looked at the TEAM section on the far right. The terms here were familiar to him: LEADER, TEAM BUILDER and SELF-DIRECTED TEAMS. SELF-DIRECTED was a term that had always confused Jack.

Next he read the definition at the top of the map: ABLE AND WILLING TO SOLVE PROBLEMS AND MAKE DECISIONS WITHOUT SUPERVISION.

"I've heard about these team ideas, but I've never experienced them," Jack said. "Lots of supervisors at work refer to their groups of subordinates as 'teams,' but most of those so-called 'teams' are really 'collections,' according to what your map says. To tell you the truth, I doubt that a real team is even possible."

"It is possible to build a real team of INTER-DEPENDENT people, but you must take it one step at

---

* The idea of maturation from 'dependent', to 'independent' (see chapter 2) to 'interdependent' was adapted from *The Seven Habits of Highly Effective People*, by Steven Covey.

a time. Let me put it this way," Jangbu explained. "Do you think Sir Edmund Hillary climbed from the bottom to the top of Mount Everest in one day?"

"Probably not," said Jack.

"No," confirmed Jangbu. "If he had attempted to climb the entire mountain in one day, he would have become exhausted, fallen to the ground and frozen to death. Yet that is exactly the mistake most managers make when they try to implement teams. They try to go from traditional management to teams overnight and, overwhelmed with the obstacles they encounter, they get tired and give up."

"That's what my company did," said Jack. "Our top management just changed the labels on the organizational chart. One day they announced that departments would now be called 'teams' and supervisors would now be called 'team leaders.' For a while everyone was confused. They knew they were supposed to act differently, but they didn't know how. After a few weeks, everyone went back to acting the same way they always had because it was all they knew how to do. That's what I did."

"Instead of trying to climb the mountain in one day," said Jangbu, "Sir Edmund Hillary established intermediate camps on the mountain and tackled the job in logical pieces. When climbing Mount Everest the

19

human body requires time to acclimate to the lack of oxygen in the air. If you take a person at sea level and instantly place him at the summit, he would be unconscious in minutes and dead shortly thereafter."

"That's pretty close to how I felt when they told me I was going to be a 'team leader,'" said Jack.

"I understand," said Jangbu. "To continue my example, if a climber takes his time and rests for several days at each intermediate camp, his body will adjust by creating more oxygen-carrying red blood cells so he can survive with less oxygen."

"Fine," said Jack, "but we've got plenty of oxygen at work, so what's your point?"

"The point is that just as there are intermediate camps on Mount Everest, there are intermediate camps on the Journey To Teams. The first column on my map, labeled Collection, is the base camp. That is where nearly every business organization must begin. The next three columns are the intermediate camps you must attain before your team will be capable of reaching their potential. Once you have built a true team, you will be able to lead that team to achieve goals that you now believe to be impossible. On Everest, the goal is to reach the summit. What is the goal for your team, Jack?"

"To be the best at what we do, so we can make a profit, keep our jobs, feed our families and maybe even become financially secure," Jack replied.

"Worthy goals, my friend," said Jangbu.

"Well, what are the two intermediate camps between Collection and Team?" Jack asked.

"I'll make you a deal," Jangbu said. "Bring me to your office tomorrow and show me what your department does. Then I will show you the next piece of the map."

Jack looked at his watch. It was nearly 11:00 p.m., and he had to be up at 6:00 a.m. "You've got yourself a deal," Jack said. "Now let's get some sleep."

The First Journey:
Individual Building

"Well, what did you think?" asked Jack. It was almost 10:00 a.m. They had just returned from touring Jack's department.

"It was interesting," Jangbu replied. "You have some people who work with their hands making metal parts and other people who sit at desks and process information on paper. They all seemed to have one thing in common: they were all bored, obviously not challenged by their work. Tell me again what frustrates you about being a supervisor?"

"It's really a combination of things, but what bothers me the most is my subordinates don't seem to want to think at work. I know they can, but I must be doing something to make them unwilling to solve problems and make decisions without my involvement. They come to me regarding anything outside the normal day-to-day operations."

"It is time for you to learn the first step on your Journey To Teams," Jangbu said as he pulled out the map he had started last night.

"Hold on, Jangbu," said Jack. "I'd like my manager to see this too. Hang on while I see if she's around." Jack jumped up and trotted down the hall. He was back in two minutes with a tall woman in her mid-forties.

"Jangbu Makti, this is Marty Washington," Jack said. "Jangbu's spent most of his life as a Sherpa guide on Mount Everest. He shared some ideas about leadership with me last night, and I think they might apply to us here at work. Show her the map, Jangbu."

Jangbu explained what he had shown Jack the night before about Collections and Teams.

"That's interesting," said Marty. "Although we sometimes refer to our departments as teams, they definitely act like collections. My question is, how do we turn them into real teams?"

23

"I was just about to tell Jack the first step when he went to get you." Jangbu said. "As you know, Everest is a very difficult mountain to climb, but I have an excellent record getting climbers safely to the top. When I take a new expedition up the mountain, I always begin the same way. The first thing I teach them is how to make decisions and solve problems as they climb. There is no trail above base camp, so they must be able to make their own. So, at the beginning, before it gets too difficult, I coach the expedition members to think for themselves."

Jangbu bent over his map, labeled the second column and added a note to the bottom of the paper. When he was done, he looked at Marty and Jack and said, "You see?"

Jack looked down at the map (see map 2). The second column was now titled WORK GROUP. He was familiar with the term COACH, but he could only guess what INDIVIDUAL BUILDER and SELF-DIRECTED INDIVIDUALS might mean, as these terms were unfamiliar to him.

At the bottom left of the diagram he read:

PROBLEM #1:
EXPECTING INTERDEPENDENCE
BEFORE INDEPENDENCE

24

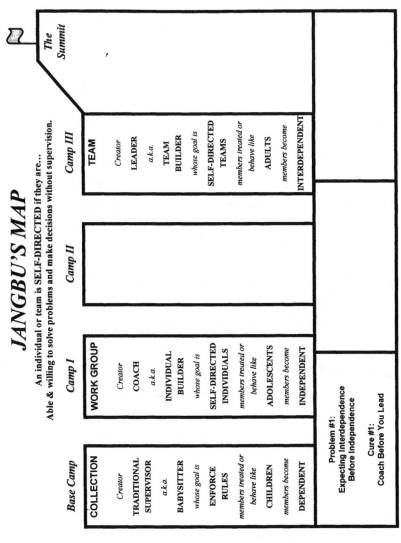

JANGBU'S MAP

An individual or team is SELF-DIRECTED if they are...

Able & willing to solve problems and make decisions without supervision.

Base Camp	Camp I	Camp II	Camp III
COLLECTION	**WORK GROUP**		**TEAM**
Creator	*Creator*		*Creator*
TRADITIONAL SUPERVISOR	**COACH**		**LEADER**
a.k.a.	*a.k.a.*		*a.k.a.*
BABYSITTER	**INDIVIDUAL BUILDER**		**TEAM BUILDER**
whose goal is	*whose goal is*		*whose goal is*
ENFORCE RULES	**SELF-DIRECTED INDIVIDUALS**		**SELF-DIRECTED TEAMS**
members treated or behave like	*members treated or behave like*		*members treated or behave like*
CHILDREN	**ADOLESCENTS**		**ADULTS**
members become	*members become*		*members become*
DEPENDENT	**INDEPENDENT**		**INTERDEPENDENT**

The Summit

Problem #1:
Expecting Interdependence
Before Independence

Cure #1:
Coach Before You Lead

MAP 2

25

Jack looked up at Jangbu and Marty. "What does interdependence mean?" he said.

"It means that people are independent but are also able to work with others," explained Marty.

Jack nodded. "It makes sense that if people at work are not yet able to solve problems and make decisions on their own," he said, "they will not be able to do it in cooperation with other people in a team."

"Yes," said Marty. "If an organization tried to implement teams simply by grouping dependent people together and calling them a team, they would not be interdependent, they would be codependent."

"Everybody counting on everyone else to do the thinking," Jangbu said, laughing. "Your people must be confident, independent individuals before they can truly be interdependent with other people."

Jack looked up. His face was more serious now. "I think we made that mistake in my department." He paused. "We organized our people into groups and labeled them as teams, and it has been continual chaos, confusion and conflict ever since. I guess they weren't ready for it."

Jangbu bent down over the map again and wrote another note.

Jack looked at the new writing:

CURE #1:
COACH BEFORE YOU LEAD

"I have to help my subordinates break their habit of being dependent on me," said Jack. "I must help them become independent, self-directed individuals who are able and willing to solve problems and make decisions before I can ever hope for them to be able to work together as a team. That's the answer."

"Not so fast, Jack," said Uncle Jangbu. "That is one of the answers, but there is another step before we get to teams, remember?"

"Well, what are we waiting for?"

The Second Journey:
Cell Building

Jack made a fresh pot of coffee and poured a cup for both Marty and Uncle Jangbu. Jangbu was telling them a story about a climber who had become separated from the team during one of his expeditions.

"Fortunately, we found the person before the perils of Everest overtook him, but it could have been much worse. I learned from that experience." Jangbu said.

"What did you learn, Jangbu?" Marty asked.

"From that point on, we tied ourselves together after

the first part of the climb. At higher altitudes, each person in the expedition is certain to make at least one mistake, and the team members must be able to help each other. The ropes are a constant reminder that not only are climbers accountable for themselves, they are also accountable for everyone in the expedition. This way the group shares accountability for reaching the summit." He paused. "You must tie your people together here at work as well."

"Um, wouldn't a group of people have a tough time working if they were all tied together?" Jack asked.

"I don't mean tied together literally," said Jangbu, "but you will need to tie their responsibilities together so that they can share responsibility for producing a complete product or service. During our tour this morning, I noticed that there are 11 different functions that need to be completed in order to make your final product. A different person in a different part of the building performs each step. They never talk to each other and they don't understand what the people before and after them do to the product."

"I can see your point," responded Jack. "There is no shared ownership. I don't feel like anyone is accountable for anything in my department. If we are late delivering an order or have a quality problem, everyone blames the people who worked on the product before or after them.

None of my people understand enough of the process to find the root cause of a problem and fix it. I end up doing all the troubleshooting, but there are too many problems for me to fix by myself."

"I can see that you understand," said Jangbu. "However, I do not know how to label the third column on my map so that the concepts will apply to you. Perhaps you can help me express them as they apply to your situation at work."

"WORK CELL," stated Marty. "What you're talking about is a Work Cell." Marty took the diagram and wrote 'Work Cell' at the top of the third column and a definition across the bottom (see map 3). She read the definition aloud: "AN ARRANGEMENT OF WORK FLOW AND EQUIPMENT SO THAT A SMALL GROUP OF PEOPLE CAN SHARE RESPONSIBILITY FOR PRODUCING A COMPLETE PRODUCT OR SERVICE OR A LARGE COMPONENT THEREOF."

"At my last company, we recognized that our people did not share ownership, and that there were handoffs between each process step," she explained. "We had to rearrange our work flow and equipment so that people could share ownership. Work cells made a big difference for our teams, and based on my experience I will have many ideas to offer concerning this part of our journey."

30

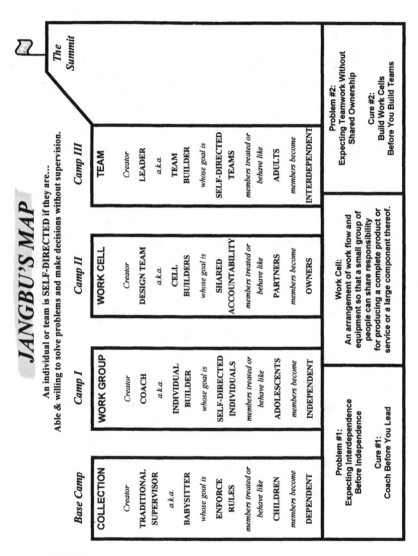

JANGBU'S MAP

An individual or team is SELF-DIRECTED if they are...
Able & willing to solve problems and make decisions without supervision.

The Summit

Base Camp	*Camp I*	*Camp II*	*Camp III*
COLLECTION	WORK GROUP	WORK CELL	TEAM
Creator	*Creator*	*Creator*	*Creator*
TRADITIONAL SUPERVISOR	COACH	DESIGN TEAM	LEADER
a.k.a.	*a.k.a.*	*a.k.a.*	*a.k.a.*
BABYSITTER	INDIVIDUAL BUILDER	CELL BUILDERS	TEAM BUILDER
whose goal is	*whose goal is*	*whose goal is*	*whose goal is*
ENFORCE RULES	SELF-DIRECTED INDIVIDUALS	SHARED ACCOUNTABILITY	SELF-DIRECTED TEAMS
members treated or behave like	*members treated or behave like*	*members treated or behave like*	*members treated or behave like*
CHILDREN	ADOLESCENTS	PARTNERS	ADULTS
members become	*members become*	*members become*	*members become*
DEPENDENT	INDEPENDENT	OWNERS	INTERDEPENDENT

Problem #1:
Expecting Interdependence Before Independence

Cure #1:
Coach Before You Lead

Work Cell:
An arrangement of work flow and equipment so that a small group of people can share responsibility for producing a complete product or service or a large component thereof.

Problem #2:
Expecting Teamwork Without Shared Ownership

Cure #2:
Build Work Cells Before You Build Teams

MAP 3

She continued to fill in the third column and read as she wrote: "A team of engineers, managers and employees called a DESIGN TEAM made the decisions about where to move equipment and who would be on what team. We also referred to them as CELL BUILDERS."

"So let me see if I've got this," said Jack. "Can I borrow the pen, Marty?" He took the map and started writing. "The goal of a work cell is SHARED ACCOUNTABILITY," he said as he wrote. He stopped to think for a moment. "Members of a work cell act like PARTNERS and OWNERS of a business within the business," Jack continued, penciling in this information as well. "That makes sense. It usually takes a group of people with different skills to produce an entire product or service. If they had all the equipment and information they needed, they would have an opportunity to manage their part of the organization like a business."

"Allow me to combine your western business experience with my mountain wisdom," Jangbu said as he motioned for the pen. Marty and Jack looked down at the map and read out loud as he wrote:

PROBLEM #2:
EXPECTING TEAMWORK
WITHOUT SHARED OWNERSHIP

"You can't expect people to work as a team if they do not have something for which they share accountability," agreed Jack. "The solution is obvious." He took the pencil and wrote:

CURE #2:
BUILD WORK CELLS
BEFORE YOU BUILD TEAMS

Jack sat down and shook his head slowly.

"Something wrong, Jack?" asked Marty.

"I was just thinking about all the money, time and effort we've spent in my department on traditional team-building activities. We went to an outdoor adventure park and fell backwards into each other's arms to build trust. We took tests to find out our personality types so we could appreciate our differences. Then we attended seminars to learn how to run meetings and solve problems."

"Sure, I remember all of that," said Marty.

"Oh, it was interesting," replied Jack, "but it was also a waste of time and money. We were not prepared to use those skills yet. I was still acting like a traditional supervisor instead of a coach, and my people were still dependent upon me to make all the decisions and solve all the problems."

"Furthermore," Jack continued, "they did not have

anything to own together, so they had no reason to work together. In the end they forgot all that they had learned because they never had a chance to use it."

Jack thought about his frustrations, and how many of them might go away if he could build individuals and give them something to own together. No wonder his efforts to build teams had been so fruitless. How could he have expected his people to start behaving like teams when he had not laid the foundations first? Jangbu's ideas made sense. He felt good. He had hope again.

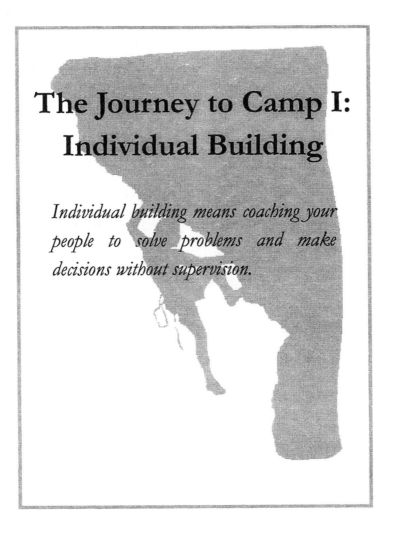

The Journey to Camp I: Individual Building

Individual building means coaching your people to solve problems and make decisions without supervision.

35

Every pair of hands comes with a free brain.

- Unknown

How To Let Go Without Losing Control

Jack arrived at work early today. He had learned quite a bit yesterday from Uncle Jangbu and Marty. Most important, he learned not to expect interdependence before independence. He knew he must first coach his subordinates to become self-directed individuals. They must be able and willing to solve problems and make decisions independently before he could expect them to work together effectively. It made sense, but how should he start?

Throughout the day, Jack's subordinates brought him problems to solve and decisions to make. He knew that he should not be giving them answers, but he didn't know what else to do.

He imagined telling his subordinates, "Starting today, I am no longer going to solve problems or make decisions around here. You are." The thought horrified him. He had been disappointed many times before after delegating tasks to subordinates. The thought of delegating everything to everyone all at once was unthinkable. A sure way to completely lose control, not to mention his job. By the end of the day he was frustrated again. Although Jangbu's ideas made sense in theory, perhaps they only worked on Mount Everest. He would talk to Jangbu when he got home.

Jack arrived home at 6:00 p.m. and could see the Sherpa had been working on his map. It was spread across the coffee table in the living room.

His eyes jumped to the sharp rocks drawn at the bottom of the space between Collection and Work Group. The space above the rocks was ominously labeled: CHASM OF FEAR (see map 4).

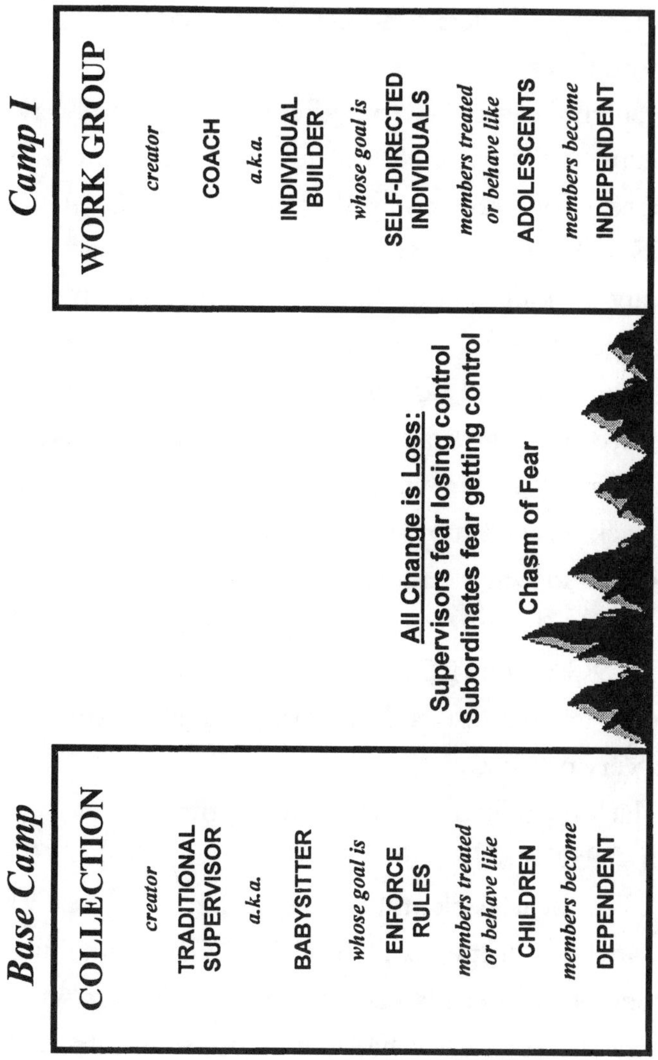

Camp I

WORK GROUP

creator

COACH

a.k.a.

INDIVIDUAL BUILDER

whose goal is

SELF-DIRECTED INDIVIDUALS

members treated or behave like

ADOLESCENTS

members become

INDEPENDENT

<u>All Change is Loss:</u>
Supervisors fear losing control
Subordinates fear getting control

Chasm of Fear

Base Camp

COLLECTION

creator

TRADITIONAL SUPERVISOR

a.k.a.

BABYSITTER

whose goal is

ENFORCE RULES

members treated or behave like

CHILDREN

members become

DEPENDENT

MAP 4

Fear. That was the emotion Jack had felt earlier that day when he thought about giving all the problem-solving and decision-making responsibility to his subordinates.

Jangbu came in from the back yard and saw Jack looking at the map. He walked over and pointed out the phrase above the rocks that read, ALL CHANGE IS LOSS. "Fear of loss is a normal part of change," he said. "Transforming a collection into a work group is a huge change, a reversal of roles. You've made all the decisions to this point, and now you must stop. Your people have avoided making decisions, and now they will take on the responsibility. This will be a big change for everyone."

Jack looked up at him sideways. "I can certainly understand why a supervisor would be afraid," he said as he pointed out the phrase, SUPERVISORS FEAR LOSING CONTROL. "I don't have confidence that my people will get things done right, if at all. I could lose my job very quickly."

Jack looked down at the next phrase, SUBORDINATES FEAR GETTING CONTROL. He tilted his head back and laughed. "What they really fear is losing their scapegoat," he said. "When anything goes wrong now, I get blamed because I'm the one who made the decision. If they had the responsibility to make the decisions and solve the problems, they'd be afraid of

getting blamed if they made a mistake. Just as I fear losing control, they fear getting control because with control comes responsibility - and after responsibility comes accountability."

"It seems to me that supervisors and employees could become paralyzed by their fears and hesitate to take even the first steps toward teams," Jangbu suggested knowingly.

"That's exactly how I felt today," Jack said.

"I can understand that," Jangbu said. "You can see why I call the space between collection and work group The Chasm of Fear."

"Jangbu, I understand the fears that stand in the way of making this change," Jack said, "but what do I do about it? I really want to make this change happen."

"Jack," Jangbu began, "if you were on a hike in the mountains and you were confronted with a wide chasm, what would you build to cross that chasm?"

"That's easy." Jack said. "A bridge."

"That is correct. There is a bridge over the Chasm of Fear. Look." Jangbu drew a bridge on the map (see map 5). "This is not a physical bridge, but an analogy for a new expectation you must make of your subordinates."

Jangbu again bent over the map and read as he wrote,

41

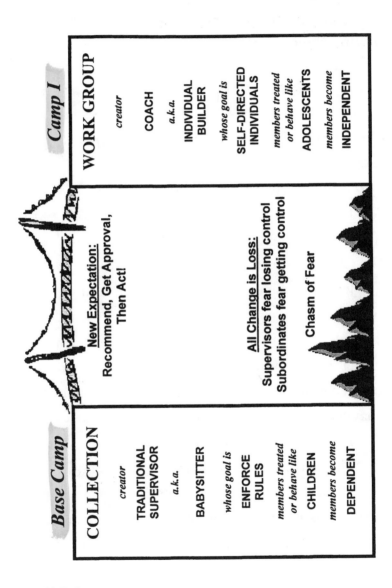

Camp I

WORK GROUP

creator

COACH

a.k.a.

INDIVIDUAL BUILDER

whose goal is

SELF-DIRECTED INDIVIDUALS

members treated or behave like

ADOLESCENTS

members become

INDEPENDENT

New Expectation:
Recommend, Get Approval,
Then Act!

All Change is Loss:
Supervisors fear losing control
Subordinates fear getting control

Chasm of Fear

Base Camp

COLLECTION

creator

TRADITIONAL SUPERVISOR

a.k.a.

BABYSITTER

whose goal is

ENFORCE RULES

members treated or behave like

CHILDREN

members become

DEPENDENT

MAP 5

"RECOMMEND, GET APPROVAL, THEN ACT*.
What do you think that means, Jack?"

Jack thought about it. "Well, at this point, when my
people find a problem that needs to be solved or a
decision that needs to be made, their preferred choice is
to ignore it completely and wait for me to find it and tell
them what to do. Their second choice is to come to me
with the problem and ask me what to do. They never
come to me with a recommendation. This new
expectation would be a big change."

"Do you think it would work for you?" Jangbu asked.

Jack thought about that. "Well, if they had to come
to me for approval before taking action, I suppose there
would not be any chance of my losing control. If I
didn't like the recommendation I would just withhold my
approval."

"And your subordinates would not feel like they were
getting control." Jangbu added. "Once you give approval,
you are still accountable for the result."

"Right," Jack agreed. And then he stopped and
frowned. "So, aren't we right back where we started with
me in control and my subordinates dependent upon
me?"

---

* Adapted from *Managing Management Time*, by William Oncken, Jr.

43

All change, even the most longed for, has its melancholy. For what we leave behind is part of ourselves. We must die to one life before we can live to another.

- Anatole France

Jangbu leaned back in his chair, raised an eyebrow at Jack and waited.

Jack sat for a moment with his elbows on his knees and his chin in his hands. Looking at the map and thinking to himself he finally said, "Well, in order for my subordinates to come up with recommendations, they have to think about them first. The bridge forces them to think without risk to me or themselves."

"But, Jack," interjected Jangbu with a sly smile on his face, "won't it take twice as long to solve problems and make decisions as it used to?"

"Maybe at first," Jack replied. "But I'll be making an investment that will give me a huge return in the future, because someday I can let them step off the other side of the bridge and into a work group."

"How so?" prompted his uncle.

"If they keep coming to me with good recommendations time after time, my fear of losing control will go away," said Jack. "Eventually I will feel comfortable trusting them to use their judgment to make decisions without getting my approval first."

"And eventually your people will lose their fear of getting control," Jangbu added. "If you give them your approval time after time, they will gain confidence in their own ability to make decisions and solve problems at work."

"This looks like a great bridge," Jack said. "It will take my department where we want to go and keep us safe along the way."

"You need to build a Bridge of Confidence," said Jangbu.

"Yes, I must build my confidence in them and their confidence in themselves," Jack concluded.

The Socratic Method

Jangbu stared at the metal trays behind the protective glass. His lunch choices were soggy fried fish sticks, mushy peas, greasy French fries or pizza that looked like cardboard. What I wouldn't give for some freeze-dried beef jerky, he thought to himself. He always thought the food was bad when he worked on Mount Everest, but this was disgusting. He wished Jack had time to go out for lunch. The company cafeteria was an awful place to meet.

He bypassed the hot food and looked in the cooler. Yogurt. That he could eat. He pulled out three containers and placed them on his tray. Jack was waiting at the register with a plate of cardboard pizza.

"Thanks for lunch," Jangbu managed to say without choking.

"Sure," said Jack. "I'm glad you could come in today. The Bridge of Confidence seems to have some holes in it. It is not working as well as I thought it would."

"So what went wrong?"

Jack frowned. "I tried everything we learned, but when people came to me with recommendations I wasn't comfortable approving, I couldn't figure out how to help them improve their ideas without turning them off. When I told them 'no', they got upset with me. When I offered alternatives, they resisted. What can I do?"

"On Everest we borrow wisdom from Socrates, the ancient Greek philosopher," Jangbu answered.

"What does Socrates have to do with Mount Everest?" asked Jack.

Jangbu took out his map and a pen. Underneath the Bridge of Confidence he wrote (see map 6):

USE THE SOCRATIC METHOD.

"I think that this is the solution to your problem, Jack," said Jangbu.

"I have no idea what the Socratic Method is," said

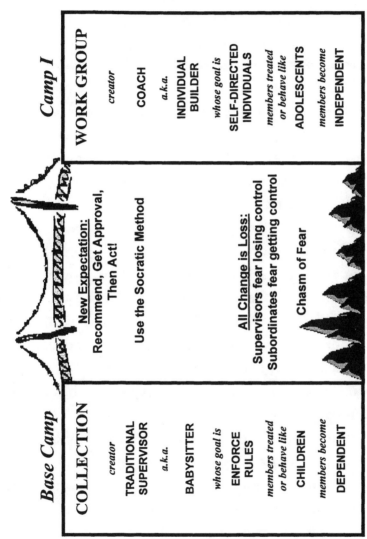

Base Camp

COLLECTION

creator

TRADITIONAL
SUPERVISOR

a.k.a.

BABYSITTER

whose goal is

ENFORCE
RULES

*members treated
or behave like*

CHILDREN

members become

DEPENDENT

New Expectation:
Recommend, Get Approval,
Then Act!

Use the Socratic Method

All Change is Loss:
Supervisors fear losing control
Subordinates fear getting control

Chasm of Fear

Camp I

WORK GROUP

creator

COACH

a.k.a.

INDIVIDUAL
BUILDER

whose goal is

SELF-DIRECTED
INDIVIDUALS

*members treated
or behave like*

ADOLESCENTS

members become

INDEPENDENT

MAP 6

49

Jack quickly.

Jangbu said, "Socrates was much more than a philosopher; he was a teacher. He taught his students using a technique that became known as the Socratic Method, which means to teach by asking questions."

"I remember something about that now," said Jack. "Law schools use the Socratic Method to teach their students. Professors ask students questions about cases they've been assigned to read. The Socratic Method is supposed to teach students how to think better."

"Isn't that what you want to do with your subordinates?" asked Jangbu.

"Sort of," Jack nodded. "But I don't want them to learn about the law. I want them to learn how to solve problems and make decisions at work."

"You must use the Socratic Method when your subordinates come to you with a recommendation that you cannot approve," his uncle suggested. "If you ask them questions about work-related problems and decisions, they will learn to think on their own."

"Yes," agreed Jack. "I think that might work. Instead of saying 'no' or offering my own alternatives, I could ask them questions to help them recognize and understand the weak points of their recommendations and how to fix them. That way they can improve the idea until I can approve the idea."

"As a matter of fact," continued Jangbu, "I think you should ask questions about their recommendation even if you intend to approve it as-is. The idea is to get them to think at work, right? If you only ask questions when you disapprove of their idea, won't they get suspicious? Give them a chance to show you what and how they are thinking by using the Socratic Method. You will make them feel confident by taking an interest in their ideas."

Jack was smiling now. "OK, I'll try it first thing tomorrow."

CLIMBING TIPS

1. If you are not sure which questions you should ask your subordinates about their recommendations, try asking questions that begin with the words Who, What, When, Where, Why, and How. I will give you some examples in the next chapter.

2. Some of the information your subordinates will need to make good decisions cannot be communicated effectively using questions. It is okay to give them facts or explain policies, but be balanced about the

51

facts you present and do not try to influence their thinking.

3. A common mistake made when a supervisor disagrees with a subordinate's recommendation is to offer alternatives. Don't do it. If you do, you are doing the thinking, not your subordinate. If your subordinate is trying to avoid responsibility, he will quickly agree to one of your suggestions and blame you if it fails.

4. Coaching takes patience. During this process you should not be overly concerned with the quality of any one decision. The goal is to get your people thinking clearly so that eventually they make dozens of good decisions every day. If you push their decision making in one direction or the other, you will slow down the overall process. They will know you are doing it and will become more concerned with pleasing you than thinking on their own. That is traditional supervision, not coaching.

Socratic Questions

Jack leaned back in his chair and stretched. He was enjoying using the Socratic Method, and his employees were excited to talk to him about their ideas. He had already had two great conversations today that led to improved recommendations. That made him and his employees happy.

"Jack!"

He looked up at his open doorway. It was Marty.

"Hi, Marty," said Jack. "What's happening?"

"You are, my friend!" She replied. "Your department has been performing much better. Way to go. Uncle

53

Jangbu's advice must have helped. What have you been doing?"

"Well, the latest idea I've been using is called the Socratic Method," explained Jack. "Instead of telling my people how to solve problems, I use questions to get them to think about how to do it themselves. They seem to enjoy doing the thinking."

Marty chuckled. "Jack, my boss has been using the Socratic Method with me for years. Every time I bring him a recommendation he asks me the same questions. I'm at the point now where, as I climb the stairs to his office to discuss a recommendation, I ask myself those same questions. Sometimes I ask myself a question that I can't answer. When that happens I turn around and go back to my office until I figure it out. When I talk to him I want to be prepared; I want to have all my bases covered because that makes me look good. And that's what he wants, too."

"Wow," said Jack. "It would be great if my people would ask themselves all the right questions before they get to my office. That would be even less work for me to do."

"You've got the idea, Jack," said Marty. "I don't want you to work too hard. I just want results, and lately you have been delivering them. The purpose of the Socratic Method is to teach your people how to think more effectively. Your aim should be to condition them to ask themselves all the right questions before they get to you."

"Do you have any questions I could use?" asked Jack.

"Sure," said Marty. "Let's brainstorm some right now."

Jack grabbed a legal pad, and they generated a list of questions. Here is their list:

- What other alternatives did you consider before choosing this one?
- What are three things that could go wrong with this recommendation?
- What is your contingency plan in case this idea does not work?
- What is the worst thing that could happen if we implement this idea?
- Is there anyone you did not consult who might be impacted by this recommendation?
- What might be our next step after this recommendation is implemented? The next step after that?
- Is there a way to get the same results with less investment?
- Are we making enough of an investment to get the level of quality we need when we implement this recommendation?

- What impact (positive or negative) does this recommendation have on our customers and suppliers?
- How long will it take to implement this recommendation and see results?
- Are there any constraints or obstacles keeping you from recommending an even better alternative?
- What measures will you use to determine the success of this recommendation?
- How could we test or pilot this recommendation on a small scale before we fully implement it?
- Who else needs to be involved in making or implementing this decision?
- What is your second best alternative, and why didn't you choose it?
- How will this recommendation affect departments other than ours?

"I'm sure I'll think of more questions as I use the Socratic Method," said Jack.

"If you ask your subordinates a consistent set of questions every time they come to you with a recommendation, they will start asking themselves the same questions before they get to you," Marty said. "The main idea is to get your subordinates talking to you. Then be sure to listen to them attentively. Your people will enjoy telling you about their ideas and will trust you more because you listened. While talking over their ideas with you, they will think of ways to improve them. That's the whole idea of the Socratic Method."

We will carry the wounded, but we will shoot the stragglers.

- The President of Hallmark Greeting Cards as he announced a major reorganization of his company

Angels, Darksiders and Fence-sitters

Jack leaned back in his chair, thinking about the last few weeks. Most of what Jangbu had taught him was working very well. Jody, one of his subordinates, was a good example. Her recommendations were not always acceptable at first. However, when he used the Socratic Method with her, she thought carefully about his questions and either explained her thinking process to him or modified her recommendation to make it workable.

He had found it difficult to let go of his preconceived ideas about how to solve problems and make decisions in his department, but when he gave Jody room to think for herself, she surprised him with some very creative approaches. He found that he was getting more satisfaction out of her success than he used to get out of solving all the problems and making all the decisions on his own. And Jody really seemed to be enjoying her job.

Three more of his 32 subordinates, Jim, Jason and Jill, seemed to be reacting in the same way as Jody, taking the initiative to bring him recommendations whenever they found problems to solve or decisions to make. They too seemed happier at work.

However, three other subordinates really worried him. Bart, Becky and Bob rolled their eyes and shook their heads when Jack announced his new expectation that they start to think at work. He talked to each of them several times to explain his new expectation and to remind them that he expected their full support. His attempts at persuasion seemed to have little impact. Yesterday at lunch he overheard them talking about him to his other subordinates.

Bart had said, "He's just trying to get us to do his job."

Becky had agreed, "We aren't paid to think at work,

so why should we?"

Bob concluded their argument by saying, "Just ignore him. This will go away like every other management initiative around here."

Their attitudes infuriated Jack.

His remaining 26 subordinates were noncommittal. They seemed cautious, but they continued to do their work the way they always had, putting in their time and rushing home at the end of the day. It was as if they were waiting for someone or something to push them in one direction or the other.

Jack was tired of waiting. As much as he enjoyed seeing Jody, Jim, Jason and Jill take on responsibility for thinking at work, he knew that he wouldn't get the results he was after unless he could get the whole team pulling in the same direction. It was clear that Bart, Becky and Bob were pulling in the opposite direction and were having as much (or more) influence on the uncommitted majority as he was. He was losing patience with them and with himself.

This whole Journey To Teams seemed stalled. Why couldn't he convince them? What was he doing wrong? He stood up and paced back and forth in his office.

"Jack, what on earth are you thinking about?"

He turned quickly to his door. It was Marty.

"Come on in. I'll tell you all about it," he said. They

sat down and he shared his frustrations with her while she listened carefully.

"I understand what you are saying, Jack," Marty said. "Throughout my career I have had my share of great subordinates, but I've had others who were a real pain in the neck. I never did learn the secret of getting them excited about the changes we were making in my department. I wonder if this is a problem Jangbu ever experienced on Mount Everest?"

"I don't know," admitted Jack. "Why don't we call him?"

Five minutes later, Jack had Jangbu on the speakerphone.

"Hello, my friends," he said. "I assume that because the two of you are calling me from work that you are seeking more mountain wisdom?"

"We sure are," Jack said. Quickly he explained the problem that he and Marty had been discussing. "Is this a problem you ever encountered on Mount Everest?"

"Jack, what do you think I would do if I had a climber who did not want to go up the mountain and actively worked against the team?" Jangbu asked. "Do you think I would keep him tied to us?"

"No, of course not," Jack answered. "He would hold back the rest of the group and stop them from getting to their goal."

"That is right," said Jangbu. "Take out your copy of the map and write this down:"

THE 10-80-10 RULE
- 10% ANGELS
- 80% FENCE-SITTERS
- 10% DARKSIDERS

Jack looked at what he had just written on the map (see map 7). Then he started to nod. "I think I understand what this means," he said. "Ten percent of the people who work for me are Angels. They understand the advantages of the changes I am trying to make. Not only do they support these changes in front of my face, they also try to convince their peers that they should participate too. On the other hand, another 10 percent of my team are definitely Darksiders. They are actively trying to convince the other people on my team to pull against the changes I'm trying to create."

"That's right, Jack," said Jangbu.

"I bet I know who the fence-sitters are," said Marty. "They are the ones who are playing it safe. They won't commit until they see who wins. And when one side

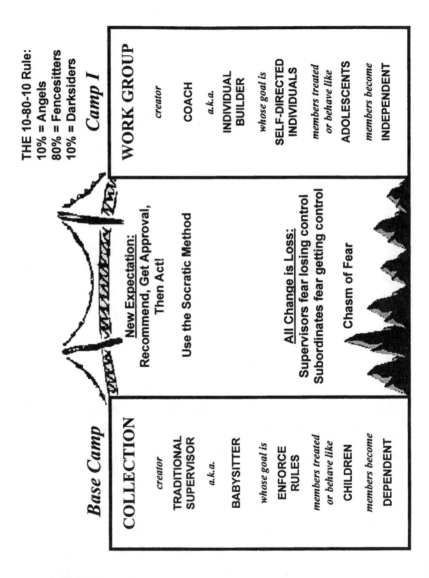

THE 10-80-10 Rule:
10% = Angels
80% = Fencesitters
10% = Darksiders

Camp I

WORK GROUP

creator

COACH

a.k.a.

INDIVIDUAL BUILDER

whose goal is

SELF-DIRECTED INDIVIDUALS

members treated or behave like

ADOLESCENTS

members become

INDEPENDENT

New Expectation:
Recommend, Get Approval, Then Act!

Use the Socratic Method

All Change is Loss:
Supervisors fear losing control
Subordinates fear getting control

Chasm of Fear

Base Camp

COLLECTION

creator

TRADITIONAL SUPERVISOR

a.k.a.

BABYSITTER

whose goal is

ENFORCE RULES

members treated or behave like

CHILDREN

members become

DEPENDENT

MAP 7

wins they will jump on the winning side and claim that they were there all along."

"That is correct," said Jangbu. "If you do not deal effectively with the Darksiders by either causing them to change or removing them from your organization, on what side do you think the fence-sitters will fall?"

"They'll fall on the darkside," said Marty. "It's easier for them because they can avoid the pain and anxiety of changing. And why should they change if there are no negative consequences for ignoring you?"

"Why would we keep someone tied to our team here at work if they don't want to come along on the Journey To Teams," said Jack.

"So, how do we deal with the Darksiders?" Jack asked.

"On Everest, we'd untie them and send them down the mountain," said Jangbu, "but that won't work for you."

"We will use our Progressive Counseling Process," said Marty. "It consists of three steps. The first step is called a verbal warning. The supervisor tells the subordinate exactly what expectations are not being met, exactly how the subordinate needs to change and the consequences of either choice. Although this first step is called a verbal warning, the supervisor must still document the conversation in writing and store it in the subordinate's personnel file."

"What if the subordinate improves his behavior after the verbal warning?" asked Jack.

"He will continue to be a member of the team," answered Marty. "However, the documentation will remain in his file for a probationary period of several months. If he doesn't change his behavior after the verbal warning, the supervisor moves to the next step called a written warning. The written warning is similar to the verbal warning, but this time the subordinate sees it in writing, which increases the seriousness of the situation for him."

"And what if the subordinate still does not want to change?" asked Jack.

"The last step is called the final warning, followed by termination if no change occurs," explained Marty.

"It seems to me," said Jangbu, "that throughout these steps the subordinate is aware of the consequences. If he is terminated he can't blame you. He terminated himself."

"That takes a lot of pressure off me," said Jack. "All I am doing is communicating the facts and the choices to the person."

"There are two purposes for the Progressive Counseling Process," Marty said. "The first is to give the subordinate a chance to change. You will find that one-third will change, one-third will quit and the other third will have to be terminated. The second purpose is to reduce the probability that your ex-subordinate will sue your company for wrongful termination."

"Well, Jack," asked Jangbu, "what are you going to do now?"

Jack looked at Marty. "I am going to give the Darksiders a chance to change, but if they don't, I am going to remove them from my team."

"Good for you, Jack," replied Marty. "Don't punish yourself and the rest of your team for the sake of a few selfish people who are not willing to change. Many organizations out there still want order-taking robots instead of people who can think for themselves. Let them work at those places."

CLIMBING TIPS

Steven Covey, in his book, *Principle-Centered Leadership*, wrote: "In order to empower a person, he must be trustworthy, and trustworthiness requires two components: character and competence."

To his words I add the following: A coach's job is to

build competence, not character.

Parents can shape a child's character, but only a combination of the hard knocks of life and the hand of God can change an adult's character. Many supervisors spend the majority of their time trying unsuccessfully to "save" a subordinate of poor character. Meanwhile, the rest of the individuals on the team are the ones who really deserve the coach's time. Deal with your Darksiders fairly, but efficiently. Don't let them hold you or the rest of your people back.

Follow-through:
The Magic of Action Items

Jack was amazed at how many more smiles he saw at work lately. Every time one of his people discovered a problem, they would come to him with their recommended solutions. They seemed to be really enjoying these challenges. He used the Socratic Method every time and asked questions that began with Who, What, Why, Where, When and How. Many people even had the answers figured out in their heads before they got to him.

His daydreaming was interrupted suddenly by a knock on his open door. Thad strolled in and plopped himself down in the chair on the other side of Jack's desk.

"We're still having that problem with the customer I.D. numbers," he said. "I thought you told us that Ted was going to fix that. I just talked to a very upset customer who said that a job he requested should have been done two days ago. We checked the file and found out that we dropped the ball because of the I.D. numbers again."

"I thought he took care of that a week ago," replied Jack. "I wonder what happened?"

A week ago, Ted had come to him with a terrific recommendation to solve a problem they were having with their customer paperwork. Whenever someone in the department received a service request from a customer, the first step was to assign a unique identification number for that job. The I.D. numbers were listed in a spreadsheet that could be accessed from any computer on the network. Whenever someone needed a new number, they would go to the nearest computer, open up the spreadsheet, copy the next available number onto the paperwork, and type the customer's name to the right of the number.

The system seemed to work smoothly until several

team members discovered that the same numbers were sometimes being used more than once. At first this caused some conflicts because some of Jack's people thought others were deliberately writing over the names they had previously written in the spreadsheet. Jack called a meeting with the people involved, and they quickly discovered that no one had any reason to do that. That was when Ted spoke up.

He explained that if two people were using the spreadsheet at the same time they would not be aware of the changes the other person was making. The changes made by the last person to log off the computer would overwrite the changes made by the first person to log off. As a result, two customers would have the same I.D. number on their paperwork.

Neither Jack nor anyone else in the room had any idea that Ted knew so much about computers. They just stared at him until someone asked, "Well, can we fix the problem?"

"The solution is simple. All we need to do is change the access rights to the spreadsheet so that only one person can make changes at a time," he explained. "Others can see the spreadsheet, but they won't be able to make changes until the first person logs off."

"And you know how to do that?" Jack had asked.

"Sure," Ted had replied. "No problem."

When everyone had finished congratulating Ted on his idea the meeting ended. The problem was solved. At least Jack thought so until Thad walked into his office.

"I'll go talk to him and find out what happened," Jack told Thad.

Jack found Ted working frantically on some paperwork at his desk. "Ted, remember that problem with the spreadsheet?" Jack asked. "Did you ever get a chance to implement your solution?"

Ted looked up. "Um, no. Actually I didn't," he replied. "I guess I got busy with some other priorities and I forgot. Sorry. I'll do it right now."

Jack thanked him and walked back to his office thinking about the last few weeks. Many of his people had brought him recommendations, but it seemed like he always had to remind people to actually implement them. The Bridge of Confidence had certainly worked wonders in getting people to think of great ideas, but what good was a great idea without implementation?

He'd have to ask Jangbu about this problem tonight. It would be his last chance for a while. Jangbu was leaving for Nepal tomorrow and tonight was his goodbye party.

"A toast to Jangbu!" said Marty. They all raised their glasses.

"It has been great having you around, Uncle Jangbu," said Jack.

Jangbu looked around the table at Jack, Nancy, Marty and Marty's husband Jeff. "Thank you all for your hospitality, and for allowing me to be part of your lives for the past two months. It has been a wonderful visit. I hope I will be able to return again soon and next time for good."

"For good?" Jack asked. It was the first time he had heard Jangbu talk about permanently moving to the United States.

"Yes, Jack," Jangbu smiled. "Everest is too tall for me at my age. This will be my last climbing season. Maybe I can help more companies like yours in America."

"That would be great," said Marty.

"In the meantime," said Jack, thinking about his day, "I have another problem for you to solve."

"Not until after dinner," said Nancy.

"Obviously not," said Jack.

After dinner Jack, Marty and Jangbu huddled up in the living room while Nancy and Jeff talked in the kitchen. Jack told Jangbu about his latest challenge.

"Jack, you have encountered a problem I often saw on Everest," Jangbu explained. "During a climb a group of people are working together, and each person has duties and tasks to perform."

"Sounds a lot like my department," Jack agreed.

"Here is the important part," Jangbu continued. "Whenever anyone in your department makes a commitment to complete a task, you must always document three pieces of information. If you don't, the task will probably not be completed. The three pieces of information are:

1. A specific description of the task (WHAT).
2. The due date for the task (WHEN).
3. The name of the person responsible for completing the task (WHO).

"I called these tasks *Action Items*, and wrote the WHAT, WHEN, and WHO for each Action Item on a removable sticky-note. Then I stuck them in my notebook to keep them safe. As a task was completed I removed that sticky-note. That made it easy for me to keep up with the commitments people made to me and their fellow climbers."

"I could definitely use that system at work," said Jack. "I'll make two sticky-notes for each task, one as a reminder for the responsible person, and one for me."

"That is a good idea," Jangbu agreed.

WHAT
Specific Description

WHEN
Due Date

WHO
Person Responsible

"I'll stick my notes on the wall behind my desk so that every time I enter my office I'll be able to see in a moment what is going on," Jack continued.

"And more important, every time one of your people enters your office they will know that you know what is going on," added Jangbu.

"Exactly," said Jack. "My people have been conditioned for years to be told what to do at work. I have them making decisions and thinking of solutions to problems now, but I also need to get them to follow up on their commitments. Good ideas are not enough without action. If I write down their commitments and hold them accountable to meeting them, eventually they will learn to meet their commitments at work without my reminding them."

"You understand this concept well," Jangbu said.

"First thing tomorrow, I'm going to find Ted," Jack said. "He will be the first to learn the Action Item technique."

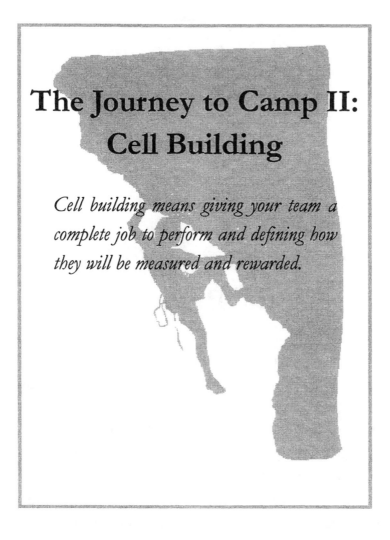

The Journey to Camp II:
Cell Building

Cell building means giving your team a complete job to perform and defining how they will be measured and rewarded.

Businesses Within
the Business

Jack and Marty sat in her office talking about all the exciting new changes in his department. Marty certainly was pleased with the results, but she was anxious to help Jack take the next steps in his Journey To Teams.

"Jack," Marty said, "do you remember when we were talking about work cells a while back?"

"Sure," Jack answered. "You helped Jangbu understand how his ideas applied to our business. I think the important point of that was shared accountability, right?"

"That's right," Marty confirmed. "Now look at the map Jangbu made for us." Marty reached into her desk and pulled out a copy of the map. Jack noticed that she had added some words (see map 9).

"GIVE YOUR TEAM SOMETHING TO OWN," Jack read aloud. He looked up at Marty. "I have no idea what that means. How do I give my people ownership?"

Jack thought about all that he and his people had accomplished in the past six months. He had finally transformed his Collection into a Work Group. He had led them safely across the Chasm of Fear, built the Bridge of Confidence and used the Socratic Method to teach his people to think independently at work. He also had dealt effectively with his Darksiders by either causing them to change or removing them from his team.

"Jack," Marty said, interrupting his daydreaming, "I know you are very happy with how well your department is performing. You are now a Coach instead of a Babysitter. But according to Jangbu's map, you are only one-third of the way to having real Teams. Is there another level that your people could reach? Are they really able to solve all the problems and make most of the decisions in your department, or are you still too involved in the problem-solving and decision-making process?"

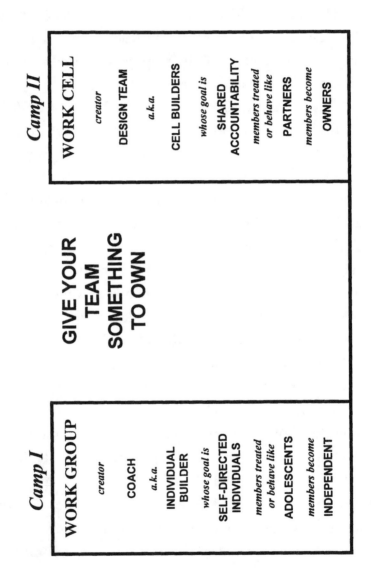

GIVE YOUR TEAM SOMETHING TO OWN

Camp I

WORK GROUP

creator

COACH

a.k.a.

INDIVIDUAL BUILDER

whose goal is

SELF-DIRECTED INDIVIDUALS

members treated or behave like

ADOLESCENTS

members become

INDEPENDENT

Camp II

WORK CELL

creator

DESIGN TEAM

a.k.a.

CELL BUILDERS

whose goal is

SHARED ACCOUNTABILITY

members treated or behave like

PARTNERS

members become

OWNERS

MAP 9

80

Jack thought about that. His work group was out-performing all of the other departments in his division. His people were taking responsibility for solving problems and making decisions within their narrow areas of responsibility.

However, when they ran into a problem that involved more than one person's job, he was still very much involved in problem solving and decision making. Why was that?

As he thought about this problem, he realized that his department was set up in such a way that each of his subordinates had responsibility for only one small, specialized piece of the entire process. None of his people understood enough about the entire production process to solve problems or make decisions that went beyond the bounds of his or her narrow job responsibility. He explained all of this to Marty.

"You know, Jack," Marty said thoughtfully, "when I was getting my masters degree in business management, I learned about a time when workers understood the entire process for making the product or delivering the service for which they were responsible. They were called craftsmen. As a matter of fact, until 1913 or so, most products and services were produced by craftsmen."

She paused.

"Well, don't keep me in suspense," said Jack. "What happened in 1913?"

"The assembly line happened," she replied. "It was a completely new way to do work invented by Henry Ford. He divided the work of making an automobile into thousands of small process steps and started using people as machines instead of craftsmen. Managers from all kinds of organizations, including manufacturers of physical products, providers of services and producers of information, copied Ford's production system and modified it to fit their environment. As this method of organizing work was passed down from one generation of management to the next, it became a habit and people forgot that there was any other way to organize work."

"Well, that is certainly the case in my department," interrupted Jack. "We don't have an actual moving assembly line, but each person is responsible for a small part of the overall job of producing our product."

"The problem with assembly lines," continued Marty, "or any arrangement where workers are only responsible for a tiny piece of the process, is that the work is not meaningful. When people are used as machines, or extensions of machines, their brains tend to shut off because they get so bored. They stop thinking for themselves and, as a result, supervisors start thinking for them. That is how traditional supervision was born."

"I agree that employees get bored doing one simple job all day," said Jack, "but hey, it's the only efficient way to do work."

"Not so fast, Jack," said Marty, cutting him off. "Henry Ford had plenty of problems with his method of organizing work and so has every one of the organizations that copied him."

"Let's start with quality," she continued. "According to Womack, Jones and Roos, in their book, *The Machine That Changed The World*, 'Ford took it as a given that his workers wouldn't volunteer any information on operating conditions – for example, that a tool was malfunctioning – much less suggest ways to improve the process.*' Workers learned that the top priority was to keep the work moving. If they made a mistake, or saw a mistake made by someone else, they ignored it and counted on the quality inspectors at the end of the assembly line to find it. In fact, in many mass production factories today, up to 20 percent of the labor hours and 25 percent of the floor space is dedicated to nothing but rework. That includes only the errors that the quality inspectors catch. You can bet the customers will find the problems that they missed."

---

* In addition, I recommend another excellent book by Womack and Jones titled *Lean Thinking*.

"So, if Ford's system has so many problems, why did he start using it in the first place?" asked Jack.

"You might be surprised to know that Henry Ford started out making automobiles using self-directed work teams of skilled craftsmen," answered Marty. "He knew of no other way to organize work. Eventually demand for the Model T exceeded the availability of skilled labor, and without skilled labor he could no longer use teams of craftsmen to make automobiles. The only labor force available to Ford was the immigrants streaming into the United States from many different countries. Think about it, Jack. If your workforce was made up of immigrants from many different countries, what is one problem that you would have?"

"We sure wouldn't be able to communicate very well," answered Jack quickly.

"In 1915 an internal survey at Ford Motor Company revealed that over 50 different languages were spoken at the plant," continued Marty. "If you couldn't speak the same language as your subordinates, could you teach them advanced skills?"

"No," replied Jack. "The jobs would have to be simple enough to teach them using hand motions."

"Right," nodded Marty. "However, there was a second problem with this labor force. These immigrants were entrepreneurs, not factory workers. In the countries from which they came, they were farmers, bakers or boot makers. They were accustomed to running their own businesses and hated the monotony of the assembly line. Most of them worked at Ford just long enough to save enough money to buy a farm or whatever tools they needed to go back to doing the work they had done before they moved to the United States. How long do you think the average worker stayed at Ford before quitting?"

"Maybe two years?" guessed Jack.

"Try three months," answered Marty. "If your people only worked for you for three months before quitting, how much time could you spend training them?"

"I'd have to get them productive right away," replied Jack. "I'd have to teach them very simple jobs."

"Now you know why Henry Ford invented the assembly line," said Marty. "He was forced to do it. He would have preferred to continue making automobiles using self-directed work teams of skilled craftsmen. Quality was much better, lead time was about the same, costs were less because there were fewer mistakes to fix and workers were a whole lot happier."

Jack was thinking hard now. He looked up at her and said, "So my question is why do the people in my department still have such simple, boring, repetitive jobs? They all speak the same language and they all want to work for our company as long as possible."

"That," said Marty, "is a question which most organizations today ought to be asking themselves."

"I need to rearrange the way work is done in my department," concluded Jack. "Then I will cross-train my people so they can own as many process steps as possible. Then they will be able to work together effectively as a team."

Case Study #1: Financial Services

Citibank management borrowed Ford's ideas to organize their process of transferring the ownership of stocks and bonds*. They divided the process into 11 simple steps and assigned one step to each employee to perform all day long, every day.

In this system an entire floor of 500 employees did nothing but open envelopes all day. Most employees had no idea how the work they did added value for customers. Errors were frequent, costs were too high and the process took too long.

Several years later, a new vice president led a

---

* From *Work Redesign*, by J. Richard Hackman and Greg R. Oldham.

reorganization of the department. He redesigned the work so that small teams could perform the entire process for a group of corporations. Errors immediately decreased, costs were lowered, lead time was reduced significantly and morale was much higher.

Case Study #2: Human Services

The employees of a health and human services agency in North Carolina were divided by functional responsibility. One department was responsible for childcare, another for drug and alcohol counseling, a third for job training and a fourth for housing. Specialists from each department often made separate visits to the same family, each collecting the same or closely related information independently.

This agency is now organizing its employees into cross-functional, self-directed work teams that will be responsible for providing a complete package of related services to families. This reduces the redundancy of information collection and allows human services professionals more time to discover and eliminate the underlying root causes of a family's problems.

87

Case Study #3: Manufacturing

As a manager of experimental film manufacturing at Eastman Kodak Company, I inherited a department organized like an assembly line. The work of making and testing film was divided into 10 distinct steps. A technician repetitively performed one of the steps all day, every day. With the help of a dedicated group of employees, I reorganized the department into self-directed work teams. The members performed all the process steps necessary to produce experimental film. In an industrial environment, this method of organizing work is often called "cellular" or "lean" manufacturing*. In this case, the results included a 79 percent decrease in rework, a 30 percent productivity improvement, a lead time reduction from three days to 10 hours and a tremendous improvement in morale.

Unless small groups of your people can share ownership for a definable product or service or a large component thereof, there is no reason to implement

---

* See appendix for information about the book *The Rapid Improvement Revolution*, which explains "lean" and "cellular" manufacturing in detail.

teams. If the work they do is not interdependent, your people won't need to be either.

*Never tell your soldiers how to do a job.
Tell them the results you want, and they
will surprise you with their ingenuity.*

-   General George S. Patton

Measuring Team Performance

It was a beautiful day. The warm air felt good on Jack's arm and face as he drove. The best part was that Jangbu was back in town to stay. He was renting a small house near Jack's home.

Jack thought about his accomplishments during the past six months. Finally he had organized his 32 people into four work cells of eight people each. Each work cell shared ownership for all the necessary steps to produce a complete product or service.

Two daunting challenges had made the change difficult. The first problem was that some of the equipment his department had used for years was big, fast and expensive, and there was not enough money available for each work cell to have its own machines. Sharing equipment between work cells created conflict and lots of waiting time. The second obstacle had been his people's resistance to cross-training. It was clear from the beginning that people in cells would have to learn multiple jobs to back each other up.

Jack and his people solved the first problem rather quickly as soon as they realized that each work cell did not need fast, expensive equipment. After all, the machines used by each cell would only need to handle one fourth of the number of jobs that the big, fast machines had to handle in the old system. Jack gave the high-capacity machine to one of the cells knowing without concern that the machine's utilization rate would plummet. Next he found some older equipment that was sitting idle for two of the other cells and bought one smaller machine for the remaining cell. Problem solved.

The challenge of cross-training was a human problem, not a physical problem. The resistance took many forms. Some of his more experienced people felt they had "earned their way up" to the more interesting, complex jobs after years of performing the simpler, more mundane jobs. They did not want to go backward. Other people warned that quality would suffer, repeating the phrase, "Jack of all trades, master of none." Still other people lacked the confidence in themselves that they could learn several jobs.

Jack kept pushing them to learn new jobs and hoped that eventually they would see the advantages. After a few months, he began hearing a few positive comments about how nice it was not to have to do the same job all day long, every day. Soon he found that he was spending less time solving quality problems because his people understood more about the process and could solve more of the problems without him.

Because the tasks required to produce a complete product or service were interrelated, it turned out that the more his people cross-trained, the better they became at every job. Rather than reducing their ability to produce quality work, cross-training made them feel more like craftsmen. They were able to ensure a quality result because the job stayed in their control from beginning to end.

Once the cross-training and equipment problems were resolved, the work cells started to perform very well. Quality improved because each work cell was unquestionably responsible for its output, making sure the job was done right. Lead time also improved because

93

there was no waiting time at shared equipment.

Jack was so enthusiastic about the new system that he had set up a lunch meeting with Marty and Jangbu to brag about how well his people were doing.

He pulled into the parking lot. Jack had invited Jangbu to lunch at the company cafeteria, but for some reason the Sherpa did not seem to like that idea. Instead, Jangbu was treating them to lunch today at a new Nepalese restaurant, which served the food Jangbu had eaten for most of his life.

As he walked in the door he saw Marty and Jangbu sitting in a corner booth, deep into conversation. When he walked over they did not even look up. They were both looking intently at the piece of paper between them. As he looked more closely he realized it was Jangbu's map.

"So what are you two concentrating on so hard?" Jack asked as he sat down next to Jangbu.

"Oh, just some new ideas for your department," said Marty.

Jack smiled, thinking she was kidding. Then he frowned and said, "What do you mean? Don't you know how well things have been going lately?"

She raised her eyebrows. "Jack, your department has been doing great," she replied. "But are you sure your group is performing as well as it can? I only ask because

Jangbu and I have a few more ideas that could help your department to really soar, ideas you are definitely going to want to implement."

Jack thought about this. He and his group had just finished making a lot of changes, and he was not sure they were ready for anything new yet. On the other hand, everything he had learned since he first talked to Jangbu had worked so far, so why not take a quick look? "All right," he said to Marty and Jangbu, "let's see what you've got."

Marty slid the map over to Jack. "See anything new?" she asked.

Jack looked down at the map and immediately saw the new addition (see map 10):

SHARED GOALS
SHARED REWARDS

"On Mount Everest, all the members of an expedition share a clear goal that they can see in front of them every day," Jangbu explained. "They also seek the same reward – the feeling of accomplishment that they will receive the moment they reach the summit. It is this shared goal and shared reward that binds them together as a team."

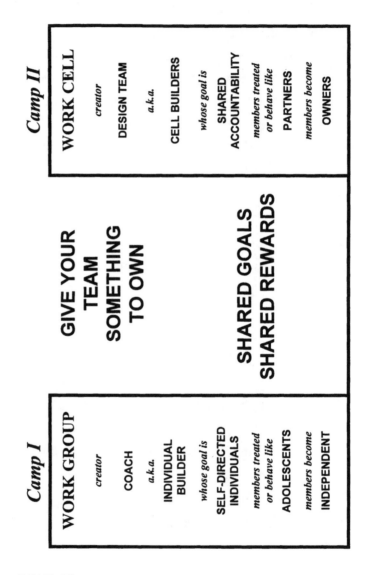

Camp I

WORK GROUP

creator

COACH

a.k.a.

INDIVIDUAL
BUILDER

whose goal is

SELF-DIRECTED
INDIVIDUALS

*members treated
or behave like*

ADOLESCENTS

members become

INDEPENDENT

GIVE YOUR
TEAM
SOMETHING
TO OWN

SHARED GOALS
SHARED REWARDS

Camp II

WORK CELL

creator

DESIGN TEAM

a.k.a.

CELL BUILDERS

whose goal is

SHARED
ACCOUNTABILITY

*members treated
or behave like*

PARTNERS

members become

OWNERS

MAP 10

"Now think about how it is at our company, Jack," said Marty.

Jack thought for a moment. "At work we reward people for what they accomplish individually," Jack said. "People compete against one another all the time, trying to make themselves look good at the expense of the team."

"Exactly," said Marty. "It reminded me of an article I read last February in *USA Today* titled, 'Why Teams Fail.' It reported that although management may be telling people to behave like team players, the compensation system in most organizations rewards people for behaving as individuals."

"Paychecks speak louder than words," Jack said. "If you want people to excel as individuals, you give them individual goals and reward them as individuals."

"But if you want them to behave like a team," Marty interrupted, "you should have team goals and reward the members of the team based on the performance of the team."

"Wow," said Jack. "Now I know why you were excited to tell me this. The timing is perfect. Before we formed work cells, there was no way for a group of people to share goals and rewards. Now that my people have control over enough process steps to produce a complete product or service, they can be rewarded for good performance and held accountable for poor performance."

"What kind of goals would they have?" asked Marty.

"Well, the main reason we are in business is to make a profit, right?" said Jack. "I think I should measure the profitability of each cell. It will be as if they owned a small business within the business, and I think it would cause them to start acting less like employees and more like businesspeople. We also could share part of the profits with them using some sort of bonus program. We'd be paying more for labor costs, but I bet in the end the company would make better profits as well."

Marty nodded. "I think everyone at one time or another thinks about how great it would be to own their own business. This would be a way for people to have that opportunity while working for a company. We could tap into their entrepreneurial spirit, and they would not have to take on all the risk themselves."

"That's exactly what I'm thinking," agreed Jack.

Jangbu lifted his hand to slow them down. "I agree that in many cases profit is a great measure," he said. "However, for some teams profit cannot be measured or profit is not the goal. Think about a management team at a hospital. They would still need shared goals and rewards."

"I agree," said Marty. "It is ideal to set teams up as

profit centers like small companies within the company. But even though our company's overall goal is to make a profit, we have teams inside the organization that cannot be measured using profit as the goal. During my career I have had the opportunity to manage both kinds of teams, and in every case we've been able to develop shared goals. I will describe two examples for you."

Case Study: Using Profit as the Goal

"My last employer manufactured outdoor grills. As the operations manager, I was in charge of arranging their manufacturing operation into work cells. We set up one cell with eight employees to manufacture portable tabletop grills that retailed for $31. A second cell with seven employees had responsibility for manufacturing mid-sized backyard grills that could be rolled on wheels. They retailed for $295. The third cell had eight employees and built grills that would be permanently installed as part of an outdoor deck. These retailed for about $2,500, depending on the options chosen.

Previously, the production area had been organized into four different departments. The forming department cut and bent all the sheet metal, the paint department painted the sheet metal, the burner department manufactured all the tubing through which the propane gas flowed and the assembly department put all the parts together into finished grills.

Today each cell manufactures its own sheet metal and burners and assembles the parts. However, paint is still a separate department that functions as an internal vendor, painting parts as they arrive from the cells."

"That sounds a lot like the change we just made in my department," said Jack.

"Exactly," agreed Marty. "Wait until you hear what we did next. Before forming the cells, the accountants had prepared only one set of financial statements for the whole company. However, soon after breaking production into cells the accountants divided the financial statements into three different parts, one for each cell, so that each cell could manage its own operation like an independent business."

"It was easy to create these reports for each cell, and the employees in each cell caught on to the idea quickly." She took a piece of paper from her notebook. "Take a look at this. It is the combined financial statements from the month before I left the company."

"Net Profit is simply Sales Revenue minus all the costs and taxes," explained Marty. "Sales revenue is volume multiplied by price per unit. Labor includes benefits of course. Materials cost is also readily available. Equipment cost is the monthly depreciation for all the equipment within the cell. Utilities and Rent are calculated based on the square footage occupied by the cell. If a cell occupies 3,000 square feet, and the entire plant occupies 10,000 square feet, then the cell is charged 30 percent of the total rent and utilities, which also gives the cell an incentive to reduce floor space. Administration is equal to the total salaries of management, supervisors and staff.

	Table Grills	Yard Grills	Deck Grills	TOTAL
Sales Revenue	$229,710	$356,950	$527,500	$1,114,160
Costs:				
Labor	23,936	20,944	33,792	78,672
Materials	96,330	66,550	201,716	364,596
Equipment	8,500	16,000	18,950	43,450
Rent	7,800	14,000	16,400	38,200
Utilities	7,313	13,125	15,375	35,813
Admin.	49,822	89,424	104,754	244,000
Gross Profit	36,010	136,907	136,513	309,430
Taxes	13,684	52,025	51,875	117,583
NET PROFIT	$22,326	$84,882	$84,638	$191,846

Each team is paid a quarterly bonus equal to a percentage of the improvement they made in their profitability since the beginning of the year. Each member of the cell gets the same bonus."

"That's great," said Jack. "I can definitely do the same thing for my teams."

"That is fascinating," said Jangbu, "but what about when the team cannot be so easily measured based on profit?"

"I'm glad you asked," Marty replied. "I've got just the example for you."

Case Study: When You Can't Use Profit As The Goal

"When a team cannot use profit as the goal, I suggest using a Performance Management Matrix*," she explained. "It is most useful when a team has several important objectives that must be kept in balance. I'll use a fun example. The President of the United States has a team of advisors called the Cabinet that helps him run the government. Certainly they can't be measured based on profitability, but they still need shared goals and shared rewards."

---

* Adapted with permission from the book *Performance Management*, by Aubrey Daniels.

These are the seven steps to building a Performance Management Matrix:

1. Brainstorm objectives

"Okay, guys, pretend you are the President's Cabinet. What are all the possible improvements you could implement to make this a better country? You give me the ideas and I'll make the list."

Jack and Jangbu hesitated a moment, and they started spouting ideas. Here is the list Marty made:

- Reduce taxes
- Reduce crime
- Protect the environment
- Improve education
- Fix the roads

"That's enough for now," said Marty. "I know there are many more, but this is just an example. Time for step two."

2. Vote on top choices

"If you brainstormed a while longer, you would have come up with 20 or 30 ideas," Marty explained. "No team can really focus on more than a few objectives. Let's each choose the one we like the most and use it in the example. Jack, what is your choice?"

"Reduce crime," said Jack.

"Improve education," said Jangbu.

"I'll pick reduce taxes," said Marty. "We chose quickly, but in a real team setting, we'd discuss our preferences until we reached consensus. Now here is what a blank Performance Management Matrix looks like."

She pulled another piece of paper out of her notebook and drew with her pen for a few moments. "We'll write our objectives in the first column."

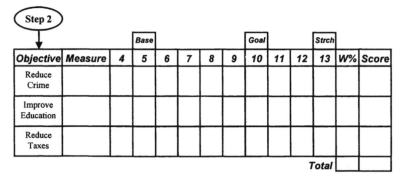

Objective	Measure	4	Base 5	6	7	8	9	Goal 10	11	12	Strch 13	W%	Score
Reduce Crime													
Improve Education													
Reduce Taxes													
											Total		

"Time for step three."

3. Define measures

"Now that we know our objectives, we need to figure out how to track our progress on improving the objectives we chose," said Marty. "Jack, you've got crime, Jangbu's got education and I've got taxes."

They each took out a pen and paper and jotted down some ideas. A few minutes later Marty asked for their answers.

"The police already have data on the number of crimes per 1000 people," said Jack. "I think we could use that as a measure."

"That will work fine," agreed Marty.

"For education, I would measure the improvement in the SAT scores," suggested Jangbu.

"Fine," said Marty. "And for mine I will simply use the average of taxes collected per person. We'll write our measures in the second column of the matrix."

(Step 3)

Objective	Measure	4	5 (Base)	6	7	8	9	10 (Goal)	11	12	13 (Strch)	W%	Score
Reduce Crime	Crimes Per 1000 People												
Improve Education	SAT Scores												
Reduce Taxes	Taxes Per Person ($K)												
											Total		

"Now for step four."

4. Determine baseline and set goals

"Now I'd like each of you to estimate where we are today according to your measure and where you think we could be at the end of a four-year presidential term if we

105

work hard," said Marty. "Where we are now is called the *baseline* or our current performance. Where we think we could be is our *goal*. I also want you to think of what we might be able to attain if we work really hard and get a little lucky. That is called our *stretch goal*."

They each thought for a minute and guessed at the numbers for their objectives. Jack was done first. "I estimate my baseline at 100 crimes per 1000 people, my goal will be 70, and my stretch goal will be 40," he said.

"Okay, now watch carefully," said Marty. "I am going to write your baseline number under the *5* on the matrix. I'll write your goal under the *10* and your stretch goal under the *13*. That is where they always go. I'll explain what the *5, 10* and *13* mean in a minute, but let's get all our numbers in the matrix for now."

"For my measure, we'd have to have a representative sample of people take the SAT because not everyone takes it now," Jangbu said.

"That's fine," Marty said. "Sometimes you have to collect data in order to get an accurate baseline, but for now just give me your best estimate."

He told her his estimates, and she wrote them in the matrix followed by her numbers.

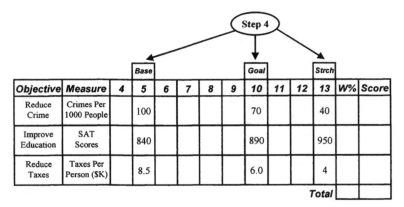

Objective	Measure	4	Base 5	6	7	8	9	Goal 10	11	12	Strch 13	W%	Score
Reduce Crime	Crimes Per 1000 People		100					70			40		
Improve Education	SAT Scores		840					890			950		
Reduce Taxes	Taxes Per Person ($K)		8.5					6.0			4		
										Total			

5. Fill in the sub-goals

"The numbers *4* through *13* across the top of the matrix are called anchors," said Marty. "They also can be called milestones or sub-goals. They act like a ruler against which we can measure the progress of our objectives."

"I think I know what we do next," said Jack. "We break our goal into sub-goals that we can measure so we can get credit as we make progress."

"That's right," said Marty. "What would be your sub-goals as you move from baseline to goal?"

"Well, I guess under the *6* I'd put 95, for *7* I'd put 90, for *8* I'd put 85 and for the *9* I'd put 80."

"Perfect," said Marty. "How about from goal to stretch goal?"

"60 for *11* and 50 for *12*," he replied, watching Marty write his numbers in the matrix. "I see what we're doing so far, but what do we put under anchor number *4*?" he asked.

"Is it possible that crime could increase?" asked Marty.

"Sure," said Jack.

"Wouldn't we want our measures to be able to track that also?" she asked.

"Yes, I guess you're right," agreed Jack. "Put a 110 under the *4* then." Marty wrote his number in the matrix and then added both Jangbu's and hers.

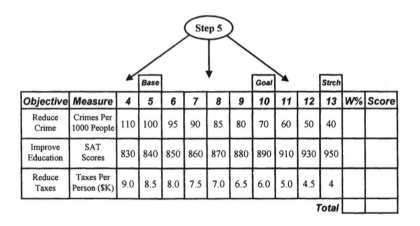

Objective	Measure	4	5	6	7	8	9	10	11	12	13	W%	Score
Reduce Crime	Crimes Per 1000 People	110	100	95	90	85	80	70	60	50	40		
Improve Education	SAT Scores	830	840	850	860	870	880	890	910	930	950		
Reduce Taxes	Taxes Per Person ($K)	9.0	8.5	8.0	7.5	7.0	6.5	6.0	5.0	4.5	4		
											Total		

6. Define weights

"The sixth step is to decide on the importance of each objective," said Marty. "We'll show the priorities by writing numbers called weights under the column labeled W%. When added together, the weights must total 100."

"So the weights of our objectives could be 60, 20, 20?" asked Jangbu.

"Or 10, 40, 50?" asked Jack.

"Or 30, 30, 40," added Marty, "or any combination that equals 100."

"So if one objective is weighted 50 and another is weighted 25," said Jangbu, "then the first is twice as important as the second?"

"You've got it," said Marty.

"For our matrix," said Jack, "I think education should get a 50. If we give people better education they might not commit as much crime."

"Okay," said Marty as she filled in the matrix. "For now let's give crime 25, education 50, and taxes 25."

Step 6

Objective	Measure	4	5	6	7	8	9	10	11	12	13	W%	Score
			Base					Goal			Strch		
Reduce Crime	Crimes Per 1000 People	110	100	95	90	85	80	70	60	50	40	25	
Improve Education	SAT Scores	830	840	850	860	870	880	890	910	930	950	50	
Reduce Taxes	Taxes Per Person ($K)	9.0	8.5	8.0	7.5	7.0	6.5	6.0	5.0	4.5	4	25	
											Total	100	

7. Calculate score

"Finally we can calculate our score as a team," said Marty. "First, we'll get the score for our performance on each objective. In order to calculate a score for an objective, we need to figure out what sub-goal we've

109

attained according to the anchors labeled *4* to *13* across the top of the matrix."

"We're at a *5* on all of them," Jangbu interrupted, "because we just started."

"Right," confirmed Marty. "Then we multiply the anchor by the weight for that objective. Jack, can you do the math for us?"

"Sure," said Jack. "Crime would be 5x25=125, education would be 5x50=250, and taxes would be 5x25=125."

"Exactly right," said Marty, as she wrote Jack's answers in the column labeled score. "Now what would be the total score for the entire matrix?"

Step 7

Objective	Measure	4	5	6	7	8	9	10	11	12	13	W%	Score
			Base					Goal		Strch			
Reduce Crime	Crimes Per 1000 People	110	100	95	90	85	80	70	60	50	40	25	125
Improve Education	SAT Scores	830	840	850	860	870	880	890	910	930	950	50	250
Reduce Taxes	Taxes Per Person ($K)	9.0	8.5	8.0	7.5	7.0	6.5	6.0	5.0	4.5	4	25	125
											Total	100	500

"Just add up the scores for all the objectives," Jangbu said. "So the total score for the team would be 500."

"Yes," said Marty as she wrote 500 at the bottom of the score column. "With this kind of matrix, you always start with a score of 500. Now I always make a graph of the team performance like this." She pulled another sheet of paper out of her notebook and drew a graph. She labeled the vertical axis from 400 to 1300 and wrote the word "start" followed by the months from January to December on the horizontal axis. Then she placed a star above start at the 500 mark.

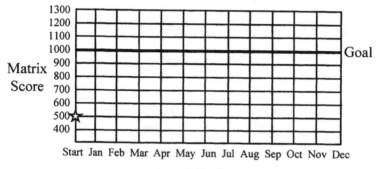

"So we'd score the matrix every month and update the graph as we make progress?" asked Jack.

"Yes," said Marty. "Let's pretend we've been at it as a team for a month and we've reduced crime to 92 per 1000."

"So we'd be at anchor number 7, right?" asked Jack.

"Oh no you wouldn't," said Marty. "No rounding on this matrix. Until you get to 90 or less, you are at 6."

"All right, so I'm at 6," said Jack. "That'll make it easy to get to 7 next month."

Marty circled 95 on the matrix and then turned to

Jangbu. "Let's say you really worked hard on education and improved the SAT scores from 840 to 880."

"Impossible," said Jangbu. "Not in one month."

"It's just an example," said Marty as she circled 880 on the matrix. "Stay with me. I am going to say that we had to raise taxes in order to pay for your crime and education improvements, so I actually went backward to $9,000 per person."

"So you are only at a *4*?" asked Jack.

"Unfortunately, you are right," confirmed Marty as she circled 9.0 on the matrix. "Now let's see you score the matrix, Jangbu."

Jangbu turned the paper to face him. "Crime would be 6x25=150, education would be 9x50=450, and taxes would be 4x25=100," he calculated, writing the numbers in the score column as he talked. "And the total score for the team would be 700."

			Base					Goal			Strch		
Objective	Measure	4	5	6	7	8	9	10	11	12	13	W%	Score
Reduce Crime	Crimes Per 1000 People	110	100	95	90	85	80	70	60	50	40	25	150
Improve Education	SAT Scores	830	840	850	860	870	880	890	910	930	950	50	450
Reduce Taxes	Taxes Per Person ($K)	9.0	8.5	8.0	7.5	7.0	6.5	6.0	5.0	4.5	4	25	100
											Total	100	700

"Correct," said Marty. "Now, Jack, you update the

graph."

Jack pulled the graph in front of him and drew a star above January at the 700 level.

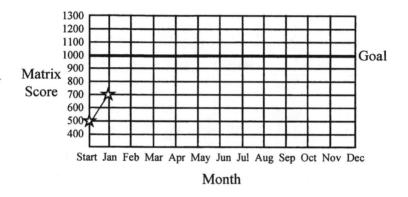

"The idea is to keep working on our objectives and score ourselves each month," explained Marty. "What is our goal for our total score?"

Jangbu looked at the matrix again. "I think we want to get to *10* on each of these objectives," he said. "So if we have all 10*s* our total would be 10x25=250 for crime plus 10x50=500 for education plus 10x25=250 for taxes equals a total of 1000 points."

"That's right," said Marty. "Would it be possible to reach 1000 without getting to a *10* on every objective?"

"Sure," said Jack. "If we got to an *11* in education, we could be at *9* in both crime and taxes and still be at 1000."

113

"Is that fair?" asked Marty.

"I think so," said Jack. "It's real life. There may be factors that are out of our control, so we ought to be able to work harder on one objective to make up for falling short on another."

"I can see how this matrix provides a very clear goal for the team," said Jangbu. "But what about a shared reward?"

"The idea is that when the team reaches 1000, they will be rewarded somehow," explained Marty. "Maybe with a bonus, maybe with a celebration or perhaps with recognition."

"This seems like a very wise way to measure performance if you can't measure profit," said Jangbu.

"If you can't measure profit, this is the best way I know to create a shared goal," said Marty.

CLIMBING TIPS

1. There are two main types of teams:

    A. The first type of team is typically called a work center team, a natural team or a self-directed team. These teams are permanent and are responsible for producing an output on a regular basis. A team of factory workers produces products. A team of janitors produces clean buildings. In most cases you will be able to use profit measures for this type of team even if the customers are other teams within the same company. For instance, a team of engineers might sell their services to teams of factory workers on an hourly basis.

    B. The second type of team is often called a project team, "Kaizen" team, task force, or quality circle. These teams are almost always cross-functional and have a specific, one-time goal or set of goals. When the goal is achieved, the team usually ends. A software development team brings their product to

115

product to market. A team of operators, supervisors and human resources specialists might develop a new training procedure. In most cases you will not be able to use profit measures for this kind of team and would be better off using a Performance Management Matrix. For instance, the leadership team at a hospital might measure patient satisfaction, adherence to budget and percent occupancy.

2. There is no doubt that making these kinds of changes in the measurement and reward system at your organization will be difficult. In fact, if you have not implemented work cells that own enough process steps to produce a complete product or service or a large component thereof, measuring and rewarding your people as a team does not make any sense. **You cannot hold people accountable for something they do not control.**

3. Remember that until you build your individuals and then build work cells, it is wasteful to invest time and money in team building. Your organization will simply not be ready for it.

Business Meetings

Jack looked at his computer screen. Using a spreadsheet, he had broken down his department's financial statements so that the employees in each of his work cells could see the amount of profit their team was making for the organization. He was not sure what to do next. He picked up the phone and called Marty.

"Hi, Jack," she answered. "How are things going down there?"

"Great," he replied. "I'm just not sure what to do next."

"All right," Marty replied. "I have a few more ideas

4 steps for round-robin brainstorming:

for you yet. Come on up when you get a minute, and I'll show you." Jack could not wait. He grabbed a legal pad and a pen and went straight to her office.

"Business Meetings," she said when he arrived.

"Huh?" Jack stuttered.

"Once you form work cells, you will need to help each cell learn to increase their profit or their score on their performance matrix if they can't use profit as the goal," she explained. "A great way to do this is by starting Business Meetings for each work team."

"How often should we have these meetings?" asked Jack.

"In the beginning, I suggest having them once a week for an hour," she said. "Start the first meeting by reviewing the income statement or the matrix for the team to remind them of their goal. Then ask them for any ideas they have to increase the profitability or matrix score for their team. I suggest using round-robin brainstorming to get the greatest quantity of ideas. Here is how it works:

1. Give each person in the room a piece of paper and a pen. Ask them to write down as many ideas as they can for improving the profitability of their cell. Allow five minutes for this.

2. Now ask each person, in order around the table, to share one improvement idea with the group. If they

do not have an idea to share, tell them to say, *pass*. As they share their ideas, write them on a flip chart. Keep going around the table collecting and recording ideas until everyone says, *pass*.

3. Ask the participants if they see any duplicate ideas on the master list. Combine these. Then number each idea on the list.

4. Ask each person to write down the numbers of the two ideas that they would most like to implement. Go around the room and ask for each person's choices, making a mark next to each chosen idea on the flip chart. Add up all the marks and underline the top choices."

"I bet you could generate a lot of good ideas using round-robin brainstorming," said Jack.

"It works great," confirmed Marty. "Now that you've got it narrowed down to a few good ideas, ask for a volunteer to take responsibility for working on each of the top choices. When they volunteer, take out a sticky note and document their commitment in the form of an 'Action Item.' Remember to include *What*, *When*, and *Who*. The *What* should be a description of what they are committing to complete by the next Business Meeting. For example, they don't have to get that new materials handling idea entirely implemented by the next meeting,

119

but they might talk to an engineer about it. The *When*, or due date, should always be the date of the next Business Meeting. *Who*, of course, would be the name of the responsible individual."

"Decide on a place for each cell to post all their current Action Items," Marty continued. "That way, those responsible will not forget their action items, and everyone can see what is happening. Be sure to remind everyone that being the owner of an action item does not mean you have to do it yourself. Encourage the owners to ask for help from teammates and staff people."

"We have a small conference room near my office that I could dedicate just for my teams to use," said Jack.

"Sounds like a good idea," said Marty. "After the first Business Meeting the agenda should go as follows:

1. Review the Action Items from the previous meeting to make sure they got done.
2. Review the latest performance measures for the cell. If they have not been updated since the last meeting, you can skip this.
3. Brainstorm new improvement projects to improve the performance measures.
4. Document a new Action Item (which are often small parts of larger improvement projects) for each

member of the group."

Jack nodded. These ideas made sense to him. If he showed his people their financial statements or matrices every week, eventually they would understand them and figure out what to do to increase their profit or improve their matrix scores. As they thought of ideas, he would teach them to document them as Action Items so that improvements would happen every week.

Jack knew from talking to customers that if his department decreased their lead time to less than one week, they could get as much as 30 percent more orders. To get them started, perhaps he would suggest that a few of his people talk to those customers. That's the idea, he said to himself. Don't give them the answer - teach them how to find it themselves.

He jumped out of his chair and walked out the door to reserve a conference room for the first Business Meeting.

CLIMBING TIPS

1. Tell the team members that you expect each of them

to take at least one Action Item at each Business Meeting. They don't need to be big efforts; they can be small tasks. If every team member takes on one small task each meeting, eventually they will add up to huge improvements.

2. Keep the completed Action Items. You can either post them in another display area or place them in each employee's personnel folder.

3. As a manager at Kodak, I coached five work cells. One cell set an aggressive profit goal. They volunteered to meet every day for an hour during their lunch break (Kodak bought the food). They used the agenda I described above for their meetings and constantly generated new Action Items. We had a silly rule to encourage people to finish their Action Items on time: If anyone did not meet their commitment for that meeting, they would have to return all of our lunch trays to the cafeteria which was three flights up. If everyone met their commitments I returned the lunch trays. I made many trips to the cafeteria, but I didn't mind. This team taped a piece of flip-chart paper to the wall in their meeting room and kept all their Action Items there. They divided the flip chart into six sections,

one for each major part of the experimental film making process, to keep the Action Items more organized. The result of all this work? The team reached their goal and had a great time doing it.

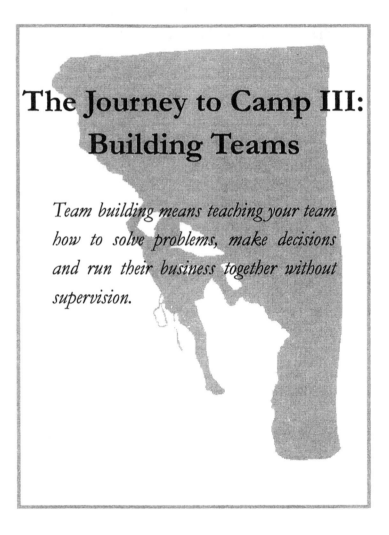

The Journey to Camp III: Building Teams

Team building means teaching your team how to solve problems, make decisions and run their business together without supervision.

How Much Responsibility Can Your Team Handle?

Jack sat at the end of the conference table, having just completed a Business Meeting with one of his work cells. Another meeting was scheduled to start in a few minutes. He was delighted with how they were going. At first, the financial statements seemed to confuse his people, but after three or four meetings they were catching on.

This last meeting had been exciting. The team was having problems with an old machine that had been

125

around for 30 years. Before they considered fixing it, they called the customers and found out that although the demand for the product that they were making was high, it could end at any time because the technology was changing. Therefore, the team decided that instead of buying a new machine, it made more sense to switch back to doing the work by hand. It would take more work to assemble each part, but they would have fewer quality problems to fix.

Jack was very proud of them. He never thought they would take on so much responsibility. It was as if they were running their own business inside the business. How far could this go, he wondered? Well, why not ask them?

As the cell team members for the next meeting came into the room, Jack bent over a piece of paper and worked on a question to ask them. Once they were all in the room, he cleared his throat and said, "I am really proud of you and the other cell teams because you have taken on so much responsibility."

"We could have been doing it all along," said Ben, one of the cell team members. "But we didn't have the financial statements and we didn't know what the goal was. We also thought that you wanted to make all the decisions. Now that you are treating us like intelligent adults, it's a lot easier to act like one."

"I know," admitted Jack. "I held you back before, and I don't want to do it again. I have a question for you. I want to know how much responsibility you can take on. If you tell me you can do it, I'll believe you and try to help you do it."

They looked at him and waited. He picked up his piece of paper and read what he had written:

> "Pretend that we just built a separate building for your work cell containing all the equipment you need to produce your product or service. Make a list of all the information you would want and all the skills you would need to learn in order to run your business on your own."

Ben picked up a marker and went to the board. He wrote the first thing he knew they would need if they had to do EVERYTHING to run their business:

- Financial information and accounting skills: ability to understand and track revenue (unit price and sales volume) and costs (materials, wages and benefits, rent, equipment, utilities, etc.)

Even before he finished writing, the other cell team members started suggesting ideas. This is what the list looked like:

- Customer information: who are they, where are they and what do they buy from us?
- Blueprints and how to read them
- Purchasing: who are the suppliers, where are they, and how can we interact with them to get the best quality and prices?
- How to identify and solve quality problems
- Human resources skills: hiring and disciplinary skills, how to decide on wages, benefits, raises
- Research and development of new products and processes. Understand how customers use our products, their future needs and our ability to redesign products to make them more valuable
- Sales and marketing: how to find and sell to new customers
- Maintenance skills: preventive and repair for both equipment and facilities
- Interpersonal skills: verbal and mental self-control, conflict resolution, time management, how to be unselfish and accept criticism, communication
- Knowledge about the competition
- How to arrange for subcontractors to do work for us when needed
- Inventory control

- Shipping
- Cross-training
- How to arrange for outside training or consulting when needed
- Regulatory requirements for safety, environment, hiring, etc.

Jack shook his head and smiled. He was amazed. His people understood much more than he had thought. They knew what it took to run a business.

"Now, Jack," said Ben, "you can't expect us to start doing all these things tomorrow. You'll have to use some of your coaching skills to help us learn."

"I know, Ben," said Jack. "It may take years for you to be able to do many of these tasks, but eventually I'll bet that you will be able to perform many of them better and faster than management or staff groups. You are closer to the problems and opportunities, and you have more collective brainpower. As a result, you will free the managers and staff people so that they can work on new projects to help us grow."

CLIMBING TIPS

The biggest mistake managers and supervisors make is underestimating the abilities of their people. Most employees are starved for responsibility and authority. Give it to them. Then give them the training (if they need it). You will be amazed at how quickly common sense takes over and how quickly they will learn.

If you try to work yourself out of a job, you will always have a job. If you try to preserve your job by hoarding information and know-how, you won't have a job for long.

- Roger Clarizio, V.P. Manufacturing, Sumitomo Electric Lightwave Corporation*

---

* At the time this book was originally published, Roger was with SEL. He has since accepted a position as Director of Operations at Krone, Inc.

New Roles for
Supervisors and Staff

Shortly after his last meeting with his people Jack was having lunch with Marty. He was worried and it showed.

"Jack, what's wrong?" asked Marty.

"I've got problems, Marty," he said. "The engineers who work for me are nervous that the operators are going to take over their jobs. I don't know what to tell them. The cell team members are doing a lot of what the engineers used to do. And it's not just the engineers who are worried."

133

He pulled out the list of tasks Ben had made in the last Business Meeting. "Take a look at this," he continued. "This list includes most of what my staff and I are doing today. By 'staff' I mean engineering, accounting, quality assurance, procurement, maintenance, human resources and so on."

"During the implementation of teams," Marty explained, "it is natural for supervisors and staff to ask themselves, 'If I teach the team members to do all of the work I do today, will my organization still need me?' I can't blame them. Some companies have pretended to implement teams in order to trick people into accepting downsizing."

"Trick?" asked Jack.

"That's the only way I can describe it," said Marty. "The management of those companies didn't know what real teams were. They never intended to develop their people's ability to make decisions and solve problems. What's funny to me is that in the end, they really ended up tricking themselves."

"What do you mean?" asked Jack.

"Downsizing almost never works," said Marty bluntly. "Most companies that downsize don't meet their cost-reduction, profit or stock price goals. These companies have given teams a bad name. Their version of teams has nothing in common with what we are doing here."

"So why are we doing teams?" asked Jack.

"Growth," said Marty.

"Growth?" asked Jack.

"That's right," she confirmed. "We are implementing teams so that we can grow, not so we can shrink. In order for this company to grow, everyone in it has to grow. That's the way it works."

"My people have definitely grown and they continue to learn new skills every day," said Jack.

"What about you, Jack?" asked Marty. "Have you grown?"

Jack thought for a moment. "Yes I have," he said. "Before I learned to be a coach, I spent all my time fighting fires. Now my team is fighting the fires and even preventing them. I've had a chance to learn new skills like marketing and accounting, and I am teaching those skills to my teams."

"That's the same way it should work with the rest of the staff," said Marty. "Teams work so well because every human being has a natural need to learn and to teach others. Teams allow people to do both continually, and that's what makes companies grow. Companies are made up of people. If the people don't grow, the company won't grow."

"It seems to me," said Jack, "that people get excited

about work only when they are learning, and they get very bored when they are not. If they get bored often enough, their initiative starts to fade and they turn their brains off. Our employees have the ability to solve most of our problems, but supervisors and staff keep taking the problems away from them. Instead, they should be coaching their employees to solve the problems themselves. By taking the problems away, not only are they stopping the employees from growing, they are stopping themselves from growing."

"Teams are a way for everyone to grow and be happy at work," said Marty. "It's like a multi-level marketing organization. The only way you grow is by helping those below you grow."

"Growth, teams and job satisfaction go together," said Jack. "That must be the cause of the big improvement in morale that comes with teams."

"Yes, there will never be a shortage of customers who want better quality, cost, and delivery," said Marty, "which means there will never be a shortage of work for people who want to take on new opportunities. That is why we are implementing teams. Anyone who wants to grow and help others grow will always have a job here."

Team Engineering 101

"Marty," said Jack, "I'm still having trouble getting my staff and team members to understand how to transition into their new roles." Jack had asked her to lunch at the cafeteria to discuss his concerns.

"Let me give you an example of how the process might work," she said. "We'll start with engineering. Without going back to school, it is likely that your people will never be able to do everything a degreed engineer can do. They will always need help in areas that require calculus or physics, correct?"

"Sure, that seems obvious," agreed Jack.

137

Marty explained the rule:

TEAM MEMBERS MUST LEAD ALL PROJECTS
RELATED TO THEIR PRODUCT OR SERVICE,
DOING AS MUCH OF THE THINKING AS THEY
CAN ON THEIR OWN.

"That does not mean they have to do all or even the majority of the work," she explained. "Think of the employees as small business owners who hire specialists like accountants and lawyers. The specialist may do much of the work, but who is in charge?"

"The owner of the business," Jack answered.

"Right," Marty confirmed. "Every time the team needs help, the engineer, acting like a coach, should teach the team some engineering skills," Marty explained. "Over time, the team members can take on more and more of the engineering tasks. Because the team is closer to the work, they will be able to apply the engineering skills most effectively. Let me show you how this progression might take place." She took out a piece of paper and a pen and wrote:

Time frame   **Activity led by cell team members**

Year 1

Redesigning the manufacturing process
Examples include rearranging machine layouts, modifying the tooling, reducing set-up times, experimenting with different line speeds, buying a new conveyor system, reprogramming a testing system, etc.

Year 2

Redesigning products for cost reduction and manufacturability
Examples include eliminating un-necessarily complicated machining operations, finding new suppliers for expensive parts, substituting common parts for specialized parts, etc.

Year 3

Redesigning products for customers
Examples include adding or elim-inating functions, changing the ap-pearance, making it more ergon-omically sound, etc.

"I see," said Jack. "This could take place over a

period of years."

"Right," agreed Marty. "In order to do these activities effectively, your people will need to learn about customer needs, product features and manufacturing processes. I recommend you use a tool called Quality Function Deployment. QFD does not require an engineering degree, but it will help you teach your team to do much of the research and thinking that engineers must do when they design good products and processes. Here are two sources you can use to learn more about this excellent tool:

- "House of Quality", by Hauser, John R. and Clausing, Don; *Harvard Business Review*. Call HBR at 1-800-545-7685 and ask for product number 88307.

- *Quality Function Deployment: How to Make QFD Work for You*, by Lou Cohen.

CLIMBING TIPS

The process of coaching your teams to take on other functions is similar to the process for taking on engineering tasks. Here are two examples:

- **Hiring**. This may be the easiest function to transfer to the team. With a little coaching, they can write the job description, place the ad or contact the temporary agency, review resumes, choose those applicants they would like to interview and make a decision by consensus on their top choice. The team has every incentive to choose the right person because they will have to work with that person for a long time, sharing accountability for team results.

- **Sales**. Your teams can make presentations to potential customers as they tour the plant, send handwritten notes to current or potential customers describing the improvements they have made recently and visit customer sites to meet with the employees who use the products they manufacture. At one plant, a team is making a video of their process to give to the salespeople while another team is developing a web site for their plant.

Do not underestimate the power of your people once you start treating them like the capable and trustworthy adults they are. And do not be threatened by their abilities. If you implement teams the right way, there will be more than enough opportunities for everyone.

"This makes sense to me," Jack said.

"Do you feel better about your team taking on their new responsibilities?" asked Marty.

"Yes, especially because we can take our time. This does not have to happen overnight," Jack said, "but it will happen."

Team Meeting
Management

"Okay, everybody just be quiet for a minute," Jack interrupted in a loud voice. He was embarrassed. He had invited Jangbu and Marty to attend one of his team's Business Meetings and this one was out of control. "You've discussed eight different ideas in the last half hour," he said to the team members in the meeting, "but you are not listening to each other and you haven't come to any conclusions on anything. Let's handle one subject at a time, okay?"

Jack was now spending a good part of his time attending his teams' Business Meetings. Usually he sat in the back and listened to the discussions, but lately he was getting impatient because the meetings seemed disorganized and were taking longer. Certain people in each team seemed to dominate the discussion while other people never said a word.

He was frustrated with the meetings and he could tell that most of his people felt the same way. Sometimes, like today, he became impatient and took control of the meetings even though he knew that it was not helping the teams become independent of him. Now that he had taken over this meeting, he ran it until the team decided on three Action Items. Then he let them go back to work. When all the team members were gone, he turned back to Marty and Jangbu who were seated in the back of the room.

"I'm sorry about that," he said. "Usually the meetings are a lot better."

"Really?" asked Jangbu.

Jack leaned on the table, paused for a moment and shook his head. "No, actually they are all like that," he admitted. "I've been trying to let the teams run their own meetings, but every time I back off the meetings get out of control."

"This situation does not surprise me," said Jangbu.

"When I led expeditions up Mount Everest, we met every morning to plan our day's climb. We also had meetings during the day to solve problems together. I taught my climbers a set of rules to follow in order to make the meetings efficient because we needed to spend our days climbing, not talking."

"Us, too," agreed Marty.

"Let's hear the ideas," Jack said.

Rule #1: Always have an agenda

"First," Jangbu said, "you have to have an agenda. An agenda is a to-do list for your meeting, a list of the decisions you want to make, the problems you want to solve, and the information you want to share. If there is no agenda, there should be no meeting. Just as effective people do not start their days without a focused to-do list, you should not start a meeting without an agenda."

"We had a rule at the company where I used to work," said Marty. "If you got invited to a meeting, and didn't have a written agenda in your hands 24 hours before the meeting starts, you didn't have to go."

"Sounds like a great rule," agreed Jack.

**Rule #2: Apply time frames to your agenda items
   and stick to them**

"The next rule is to use time frames," explained

145

Jangbu. "Let's say you've planned a meeting from 4:00 to 4:30 a.m."

"Hold on," interrupted Jack. "That might be fine for Mount Everest, but 4:00 a.m. is a little early around here, and we like to have an hour for Business Meetings."

Jangbu laughed. "Okay, 9:00 to 10:00 then," he said. "Your written agenda might read something like this:

Agenda Item A, 9:00 to 9:15
Agenda Item B, 9:15 to 9:20
Agenda Item C, 9:20 to 9:45
Agenda Item D, 9:45 to 10:00."

"I know why we need time frames for our meeting," said Marty. "Recently I read about a law called Parkinson's Law, which states 'Conversation during a meeting will expand to fit whatever size container you give it.' It's true isn't it? For instance, if an agenda has no time frames, how long will the first agenda item take?"

"Most of the meeting," Jack answered.

"Right," said Jangbu. "People tend to manage their conversations to the expectations you make. I also suggest that you have a time keeper for each meeting to watch the clock and give a two-minute warning when discussion time for a certain agenda item is running out. When participants hear the warning, they will attempt to reach a conclusion."

Rule #3: Always start on time

"The third rule is to always start on time no matter how many people are late," continued Jangbu. "If you start your meetings late, whom are you rewarding?"

"The people who come late," Marty said.

"That's right," said Jangbu. "And whom are you punishing?"

"The people who are on time," Jack said.

"Right again," confirmed Jangbu. "If you keep starting late, people will arrive later and later. Even people who are normally very prompt will start to arrive late because they don't want their time to be wasted."

"We are always waiting for people who are late," said Jack.

"Not anymore, Jack," Jangbu said. "Make it a habit to start your meetings on time no matter how many people have arrived."

Rule #4: Equalize input

"The purpose of a meeting is to get the benefit of applying many brains to a problem or decision in order to reach a better outcome," Jangbu said. "If one or two people dominate discussion during a meeting and another couple of people never talk, you will not meet your objective."

"One strategy I used to get equal input was to have someone volunteer to be what is called a *gatekeeper* for the meeting. This person's job is to monitor the meeting and become aware of anyone who is dominating the discussion. When the dominator stops to take a breath, the gatekeeper should diplomatically interrupt him and say something like, 'Joe, you really have got some great ideas today. I appreciate your sharing them.' Then, without hesitating, the gatekeeper will turn to look at a person who has not been speaking enough and say, 'Jill, I know you've got some ideas. What do you think about this subject?' This way, the gate has been temporarily shut for the dominator and opened for the person who has not offered input yet."

"That's a great idea," said Jack. "Marty already taught me a technique to get everyone involved called round-robin brainstorming. I used it in our first few Business Meetings to generate ideas."

"I've got another technique I borrowed from the book, *Robert's Rules of Order*, if you'd like to hear it," said Marty.

"I'm interested," said Jangbu. Jack nodded also.

"Robert's Rules of Order," began Marty, "is the ultimate set of meeting guidelines that is used by the United States Congress to keep their sessions on track, so you know they must be very powerful rules. In Congress, only one person can speak at a time for a predetermined amount of time."

Marty continued, "I call my version of this rule *The 30-Second Talk List.* The person who is facilitating the meeting starts by introducing an agenda item and asking if anyone has any ideas or comments. The facilitator points to the first person who raises their hand and says, 'Okay, you've got 30 seconds.' Then the facilitator writes the person's name on the top of a piece of flip-chart paper. While this first person is talking, other people can raise their hands to indicate that they would like to speak as well. The facilitator adds their names under the first speaker's name on the flip chart. When the first speaker's 30 seconds have elapsed (regardless of whether he has finished or not), he must relinquish the floor to the next person on the list, and so on. Of course when his time runs out he can always request to have his name added back to the bottom of the list."

"Very interesting," said Jangbu.

"Some of the best meetings I have ever attended have used this method," Marty continued. "People have a chance to express themselves without fear of being interrupted and they normally find that 30 seconds is more than enough time. While waiting for their turn, people must either listen or think about the most concise

149

and logical way to present their points of view. People repeat themselves less because they know they were heard the first time. Often, when a person's name is reached on the list, they will simply say, 'I agree with the last speaker,' or 'I don't have anything else to add.' In short, this method results in very thoughtful meetings in which people are actually listened to."

Rule #5: Use a "Parking Lot" to Stay on Track

"Do people ever bring hidden agendas to your meetings?" Jangbu asked Jack and Marty. "Do they ever tend to get off track and talk about topics that are unrelated to the agenda?"

"Sure they do," Jack replied. "How can I get people to stick to one subject at a time?"

"First," Jangbu answered, "assume that the people would probably not be disrupting the agenda unless they had something important to say. As soon as they have explained their concern in enough detail for you to understand it, say to the person, 'Bill, you've brought up an important point. Let me paraphrase it back to you to make sure I understand it. I think I heard you say, 'we need to open a free clinic to give low-income patients continuing care in order to reduce the demand on the emergency room.' Did I get it right?' If you didn't, Bill will correct you."

"Keep rephrasing until you get it right," Jangbu continued. "Then turn to a piece of flip-chart paper and write the words PARKING LOT at the top. Below the title write Bill's concern just as you successfully paraphrased it a moment before. Again, check with him to make sure you got it right. Then say, 'That is an important point. Although it is not on the agenda for today's meeting, I want to make sure we don't forget it. I have recorded it in the parking lot to make sure that we either: 1) handle it at the end of this meeting if we have time, 2) handle it at the beginning of our next meeting, 3) have a separate meeting just for this subject, or 4) perhaps you and someone else can work on the idea and develop a more detailed proposal that we can discuss efficiently during a future meeting.' Then, assertively let him know that you will need to continue with the planned agenda. Bill should be very cooperative at this point."

"It seems to me that would work great," said Marty. "Everyone in the meeting was exposed to Bill's concern at least three times; he said it, you said it and you wrote it on a piece of flip-chart paper in plain view for everyone to see for the rest of the meeting."

"In order for this technique to work on a continuing basis," Jack interjected, "you'd better be sure to follow up on Bill's concern by scheduling a time to handle it, or

151

he won't believe you again."

"Right," agreed Jangbu.

Rule #6: Document Action Items

"There are only three reasons to have a meeting," said Jangbu. "They are: 1) to solve a problem, 2) to make a decision, or 3) to share information. In each case, if action does not result, the time was wasted. For each problem solved, decision made or piece of information shared, your team must decide on a follow-up action and solicit a volunteer to take responsibility for making it happen. Then document this commitment in your meeting notes using the Action Item technique. Remember *What*, *When*, and *Who*: clear description of the task, due date, and owner. Review these action items at the conclusion of the meeting. Then review the action items at the beginning of the next meeting to ensure that they were all completed."

"We could put the Action Items in our meeting notes to remind the attendees of their commitments between meetings," Jack said.

"Good idea," agreed Marty.

Rule #7: Make Consensus Decisions

"You should make as many decisions by consensus as you can," advised Jangbu. "Do you know what consensus means?"

"It means everyone agrees, right?" asked Jack.

"No," corrected Marty. "I define consensus as 75 percent agreement, 100 percent commitment. That is, not everyone has to agree with the decision, but everyone has to be committed to implementing the decision."

"Marty is right," said Jangbu.

"So how do you know when to stop discussion and decide on a solution?" Jack asked.

"First, at least 75 percent of the participants should be in agreement," explained Jangbu. "Second, all points should have had a fair hearing, and those in the minority should feel as if they have been heard."

"My experience is that decisions made using consensus will not always be absolutely the best decisions, but they will almost always be better than a decision made by one individual," said Marty.

"Remember," said Jangbu, "a reasonably good decision that is implemented is always superior to a great decision never implemented because of group indecisiveness." Jangbu leaned back in his chair.

"Are those all your rules?" Jack asked.

"You have heard them all," Jangbu confirmed.

"Wait," said Marty. "I've got one more that I bet you didn't use on Everest."

153

Rule #8: Measure Meeting Effectiveness

"Jack, you should design a short survey to be completed by all participants at the conclusion of each meeting to measure how well they followed their own rules," Marty suggested. "The questions might include:

1) Did we start on time?
2) Was an agenda distributed for this meeting at least twenty-four hours before it started?
3) Were time frames assigned to each agenda item?
4) Were all agenda items handled within the time frames assigned?
5) Did we assign an action item for each problem we solved or decision we made?"

Marty continued, "I suggest a scale of 0-2 for each question, 0 = NO, 2 = YES, and 1 = SOMETIMES. Identify a place at the bottom of the survey form for the total and for comments."

"It seems like this quiz would remind everyone of the rules they agreed to follow," said Jangbu, "and show them where they may be falling short."

"Right," said Marty. "After everyone fills out this quick survey, the facilitator should collect the forms and quickly calculate the average score. Plot this percentage on a chart with scores for past meetings on an overhead or flip-chart sheet. Report to the group any obvious feedback from the surveys that explains a lower score."

"Once people get used to it, the quiz shouldn't take more than a few minutes," Jack pointed out.

"In fact, it will actually save you time by keeping your meetings efficient," added Marty. "Remember, what gets measured gets done."

"I can't wait to teach these ideas to my teams," said Jack.

MEETING MANAGEMENT RULES:

1. Always have an agenda
2. Use time frames
3. Always start on time
4. Equalize input
5. Use a "Parking Lot" to stay on track
6. Document action items
7. Make consensus decisions
8. Measure meeting effectiveness

Conflict Resolution

"So, Jack, how have your meetings been going lately?" asked Jangbu as he pulled himself up onto the rock. Although Jangbu was in his late-50s, he dragged Jack out to the mountains every month or two for a weekend of hiking and camping.

"I can't think until I catch my breath," answered Jack. "Can we just sit on this rock for a while and rest?"

Jangbu sat down on the outcropping, and the two of them looked out at the landscape below. They were 3,500 feet above a large man-made lake.

Finally after 10 minutes of silence Jack said, "My

teams' Business Meetings have been a whole lot better. Your meeting rules have been working great. I taught the meeting rules to my people and then asked one person from each team to be the meeting facilitator. I plan to rotate the facilitators to give everyone a chance to learn."

"So, all your meetings are running smoothly?" Jangbu asked.

"I didn't say that," said Jack. "Sometimes there is a lot of conflict. I want the teams to make decisions and solve problems without me, but when they have disagreements they get upset, stop talking to one another and won't work together for a few days. Then I have to act like a referee and make decisions for them."

"Ah, that is typical," said Jangbu.

"Typical?" asked Jack. "What do you mean?"

"On Everest, my climbers disagreed often," explained Jangbu. "Sometimes they became very emotional because their lives and personal safety were at stake. I could not make the conflict go away, but I did teach them methods of dealing with their conflict so that they could reach a compromise and continue to work together productively."

"Could you teach me those methods of resolving conflict constructively?" asked Jack.

"Of course," Jangbu answered. "There are two basic conflict situations your people will need to be able to deal with. The first is when someone is upset with you."

"And the second must be when you are upset with someone else," Jack guessed.

"You've got it," said Jangbu. "We'll start with what to do when someone is upset with you. The first thing you need to understand is that whenever a person is confronted with a conflict situation, the first impulse is to either battle it out or run away. This is called the fight-or-flight impulse. During this phase, a person is using his survival instincts, not his brain. As long as a person is in this emotional condition, you will not be able to resolve the conflict. For instance, have you ever had someone angry with you who seemed stuck in the fight mode?"

"Yes," said Jack. "I call it venting. They're just telling you everything they are mad about, even unrelated issues."

"I see you understand," said Jangbu. "When someone is venting, does it make any sense to try to communicate with them?"

"No," replied Jack. "If you try to talk with them while they are venting, you won't be communicating, you'll be escalating."

"Exactly," agreed Jangbu. "At this point in a conflict situation, I suggest using a technique called NSS. NSS stands for Neutral Silent Stare. If a person is venting at you, just look at them, listen to them and let them get it

158

all out of their system. Eventually they will begin to think logically and you will be able to talk with them again. They will be more open to listening to you because you listened to their opinions first."

"Once they've stopped venting," Jangbu said, "your first words should be: 'What results would you like to see out of this situation?' Why do you think that is the right question, Jack?"

"You are finding out what they want," said Jack. "Maybe you can help them get it."

CONFLICT RESOLUTION PROCESS
(When someone is upset with you)
NEUTRAL
SILENT
STARE

Then... What RESULT do you want?

"The purpose of conflict resolution is to find a way for both people to be satisfied, to make it a win/win outcome," continued Jangbu. "That takes creativity and calm thinking. As you said, the first step is to find out what they want. Unless you listen first, you'll never get a chance to use reason."

Jack chuckled to himself. The technique was so

simple and would definitely avoid problems. It would also be fairly easy to teach to his people. "How did it work on Everest?" Jack asked.

"It worked very well," Jangbu said. "As I said before, the key to conflict resolution is to get out of the emotional state so you can both use your brains."

"So what about the other conflict situation, when you are upset with someone else?" Jack asked.

"This one is a seven-step formula*," said Jangbu. "First I'll explain it, then I want you to try it with a real example from work.

Step 0:   Calm yourself. Eventually the emotion-stimulating chemicals surging through your body will go away and you'll be calm enough to think clearly. If you try to deal with the situation before you are calm, you will probably fail.

Step 1:   Say, *When you...* followed by a description of the behavior that upset you.

Step 2:   Describe how the behavior makes you feel by

---

* Adapted from *Coaching and Team Leadership Skills for Managers and Supervisors*, by SkillPath Publications.

saying, *I feel....*

Step 3:   Describe why the observed behavior makes you feel that way by saying, *Because I....*

Step 4:   End this statement by saying, *What do you think?* Then let the other person talk.

Step 5:   When the other person has finished, describe the kind of behavior you would like to see next time by saying, *I would like....*

Step 6:   Describe why you would like the person to do this by saying, *Because I...*, followed by the reason this new behavior would make you feel better.

Step 7:   Conclude by saying, *What do you think?* Then allow the other person to talk."

"Now it's time for you to try it, Jack," said Jangbu. "Do you remember the last time you were upset with someone at work?"

"Yes, it was just last week. I went to talk to one of my peers in his office, and the whole time I was talking to him he kept working on his computer," explained

Jack. "It didn't seem like he was listening to what I was saying."

"Good example," said Jangbu. "Now use the seven-step process. Pretend that I am the person you were upset with. Start with just the first four steps."

Jack thought for a moment, then started, "When you continue working on your computer while I am talking to you, I feel frustrated because I don't understand how you can be listening to what I say at the same time your attention is being focused on something else."

"Very good," said Jangbu. "Now you would pause to hear my thoughts. I might say, 'Oh, I didn't know.' Now do the last three steps."

"The next time I come to talk to you in your office," said Jack, "I would like you to pay attention exclusively to me while I am talking because I would feel like you think what I am saying is important."

"Excellent," said Jangbu, slapping him on the back. "You are a quick learner. Think about the statements you made. You expressed your feelings with nothing but facts. No one can argue with what you observe, what you feel or why you feel that way. You are taking complete ownership of your feelings. If you deliver this information calmly, you will be amazed at the reaction you will see. In most cases, it will not feel like conflict to the other person. They will not fall into the fight-or-flight impulse. Instead, they will think about what you have said and give you a logical reply."

"I have used this technique many times and each time I end up with a better relationship with the other person after the encounter instead of a broken relationship," Jangbu continued. "Notice that this technique has a chance built into it for the other person to respond before you get too far."

"That's a good point," said Jack. "I can remember a few times when I was upset with another person and it turned out that I was wrong. Step four would have saved me a lot of embarrassment."

"It has certainly helped me," said Jangbu.

"Wait a minute," Jack said. "There are many situations where this might not work. Not everyone is reasonable."

"You are right, Jack," said Jangbu. "It will not work all the time. These methods assume that both people want to solve the conflict. If they don't, you've got another problem to dig into. However, using these techniques will surely increase your probability of success."

"So," Jack said. "If I don't teach the members of my team how to resolve conflict constructively, they will never mature into the kind of team that they can be and that I want them to be."

163

"Now you really understand," Jangbu said.

SEVEN STEP CONFLICT
RESOLUTION PROCESS
(When you are upset with someone)

1. "Calm yourself"
2. "When you..."
3. "I feel..."
4. "Because I..."
5. "What do you think?"
6. "I would like..."
7. "Because..."
8. "What do you think?"

Courtship and
Team Building

"I must be doing something wrong," Jack lamented. He had invited Jangbu and Marty to talk with him in his office this morning.

"What do you mean, Jack?" asked Marty. "Your teams have been producing excellent results. Their quality is better than ever, productivity is up 25 percent, and they've reduced lead time considerably."

"I know," admitted Jack. "And I'm glad about that. It just bothers me that there is still so much conflict within

165

4 stages dev.'
of meeting

the teams."

"What sort of conflict?" Jangbu asked.

"Mostly clashes over who is going to do what jobs within the cell," Jack explained. "In some teams, members are struggling with one another to establish their leadership, while in others no one wants to do the tougher, more monotonous jobs. I keep having to get involved to make decisions for them."

"Jack's teams are maturing," said Jangbu.

"What do you mean?" asked Marty. "It sounds to me like they are struggling."

"Jack has given them all the tools they need, and he has done it well," said Jangbu. "He can't do all the work for the team. Any group of two or more people who want to be productive together must go through a growth process before they can become truly interdependent. Leaders need to understand this process if they want their teams to be successful."

"You will recognize four stages of growth, known as *forming, storming, norming,* and *performing*[*]," explained Jangbu. "As an example, let us use the oldest type of team."

"A baseball team?" guessed Jack.

"No, I am thinking of a much older team," said

---

[*] Adapted from Tuckman, Bruce W., "Development Sequence in Small Groups", *Psychological Bulliten* (1965).

Jangbu.

"How about the family?" said Marty.

"That is the one," said Jangbu. "The forming stage of a man-woman relationship is called courtship or dating. In this stage, both people are very polite and on their best behavior. They are somewhat superficial and show only their best sides. If either recognizes some sort of conflict on the horizon they will avoid dealing with it; they will put it aside and hope it will go away. This is exactly the way a group of individuals at work will act toward one another when they are asked to work together for the first time."

"I've seen that," said Jack, "but my teams are certainly past the polite stage now."

"I am sure they have moved to the next stage by now," acknowledged Jangbu. "Staying with our example, the next stage in a man-woman relationship happens when they decide to get married and begin living together for the first time. This stage is called storming, and those of us who have lived through it will agree that it is appropriately named."

"That's for sure," said Marty. "When my husband and I first shared a home we argued about everything. Until then we had been accustomed to living independently. The habits that worked great for him on his own clashed with my habits. We argued about who

167

would prepare meals, who would take care of housecleaning, who would make sure the bills got paid and priorities for spending money."

"You are on target," confirmed Jangbu. "Storming is conflict caused by disagreements about how work gets done. Teams start to storm the first time they try to work together toward a goal you set for them. Team members come from unique backgrounds and have different work experiences. They are probably accustomed to working independently, or even worse, being dependent on a supervisor to do all their problem solving and decision making for them. The point is that they all have different, and probably conflicting, expectations of how a team should work. Working out agreements and compromises about how to work together is frustrating and emotionally painful for team members."

"What scares me is that some marriages fail during the storming stage," said Jack. "I don't want my teams to fail."

"I understand," said Jangbu. "A husband and wife who are committed to one another, yet cannot figure out how to resolve their differences on their own, may decide to go to a marriage counselor for help. Jack, you will be the marriage counselor for your teams. A poor counselor tells people the answers to their problems. A good counselor acts as a neutral mediator who helps them talk to one another and develop a solution of their own. An excellent counselor teaches them processes for communicating and resolving conflicts on their own, so they can handle future problems without outside help. Like a marriage counselor, you will help your teams the most not by resolving their problems for them, but by teaching team members how to resolve conflict on their own. Do you remember the conflict management techniques I taught you?"

"Yes, I do," admitted Jack. "I taught them to my people in a meeting two weeks ago, but I guess I have to help them learn to use them."

"Every time you see them in conflict, enforce your expectation that they use the methods you taught them," advised Jangbu. "In a marriage, storming gives way to norming as the newlyweds resolve disagreements between conflicting habits. In some cases they will split up responsibilities, and in other cases they will share them. They figure out who will keep track of the finances, how to make decisions on purchases, who will cook dinner and who will do the dishes after dinner. At work, individuals in a team will norm as they find their places in the routine of getting the daily work done. After the norming stage, couples at home and teams at work will be able to perform together as a team and move toward shared goals."

169

"Then we're finally finished, right?" asked Jack.

"No," replied Jangbu. "Teams do not form, storm, norm and perform just once. Although each time will be less traumatic, they will repeat the entire cycle every time there is a change in membership or goals or as team members grow and change as individuals."

"I was just thinking about your family example, Jangbu," said Marty. "I remember when I had my first child. There was a lot of new work to be done and new roles to play. My husband and I experienced some storming as we figured out how to work together to get it all accomplished."

"I guess it's the same at work," said Jack. "If one team member leaves and another comes on board, it is unlikely that the new member will fill the exact role played by the departed member. The team will storm until the roles are redistributed."

"Just remember, Jack," concluded Jangbu, "when your team is in turmoil, it is probably not because you are a bad coach or the team members are immature. Storming is a natural and necessary part of growth. There are some teams that actually get stuck in the forming stage and stay polite, superficial and ineffective. Do not be afraid to demand results and get them to argue a little. If they never storm, they will never perform."

These ideas made Jack feel a lot better. Apparently, what his team had gone through was normal. It would just take a little time.

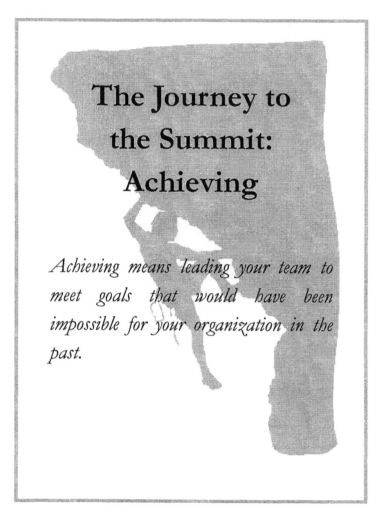

The Journey to the Summit: Achieving

Achieving means leading your team to meet goals that would have been impossible for your organization in the past.

Every noble work is at first impossible.

- Thomas Carlyle

How to Lead Your Team to Achieve Impossible Goals

Jack and Jangbu were exhausted, but in less than two hours of energetic climbing they had reached the 7,500-foot summit of the tallest mountain in the state. They could see the entire range of mountains stretched out on either side of them.

When they had caught their breath, Jangbu asked, "We have not talked about your teams in a while. How are they doing?"

"Just fine," answered Jack.

"Fine?" prodded Jangbu. "Fine does not sound very exciting."

"Well, I guess we're all a little bored," Jack said. "After all the exciting changes and growth, things have settled down. Maybe a little too much."

"I know the feeling," said Jangbu. "We all need new challenges in order to feel alive. I think that is why so many people attempt to climb Everest. They see it as the ultimate challenge. Perhaps you and your people need new challenges."

"I think you are right," said Jack. "They are performing at a high level now, but it is too easy for them."

"You must ask them to achieve an impossible goal," said Jangbu. "People want to be asked to take on challenges that appear impossible. But they need a leader with the guts to ask them."

"When you say impossible what do you mean?" asked Jack.

Jangbu defined it for him:

IMPOSSIBLE GOAL:
A goal that is so big, no one in the organization knows how to attain it.

"That sounds interesting," said Jack. "Tell me more."

"I have been studying this subject since I arrived in America, and I have some ideas to share with you."

Leadership in Distress

"I have found that throughout history most individuals and organizations attempt the impossible only when outside pressure has forced their backs against the wall, the morale of the troops is low and their freedom of movement has become severely restricted," said Jangbu. "In these cases, you will sometimes see success, but normally the odds are stacked in favor of failure."

"That's true," agreed Jack. "Most people won't do anything to change until it is too late."

"Organizations need leadership in these dire circumstances," Jangbu continued. "Warren Bennis, author of *On Becoming A Leader*, defines this sort of leadership as a state of devotion born of distress. When an organization is in distress, it is a time of great change, and change creates emotional needs in people. It is natural for people to want stability and security. When they cannot count on the world around them to remain the same, they will follow whoever seems most confident and offers the most reasonable plan for a return to stability and security. These kinds of leaders generate

generate hope and commitment in followers mostly out of desperation."

"That is the kind of leadership we usually hear about," said Jack.

"Well, you certainly hear about the successes," Jangbu acknowledged. "This type of leadership can succeed, and when it does, the leaders become heroes. In 1939, British Prime Minister Neville Chamberlain and the British people tried to ignore the aggression of Hitler and Germany. Chamberlain even surrendered Czechoslovakia to Hitler to appease him. It did not work. Hitler invaded England's ally, Poland, forcing war. As a result, Neville Chamberlain was forced out of office and Winston Churchill was able to pull out the victory, but only after great losses."

"That is a great example of how ignoring a problem makes it worse," said Jack.

"In most cases, laziness in all its forms leads to distress and then to doom," said Jangbu. "I call this first type of leadership, Leadership in Distress."

"It sounds to me as if those types of organizations only think of closing the barn door long after the horse has escaped," said Jack.

"Yes," agreed Jangbu, "and usually they never find the horse."

"Is there another type of leadership?" asked Jack.

"Is it possible to close the barn door before the horse escapes?"

"Yes," said Jangbu. "It really comes down to a choice of timing. When times are good, an organization either can pull further ahead of the competition or relax and wait until the competition passes them by. Then they must try to catch up in distress. Is it more costly to close the door before the horse runs away or after the horse runs away?"

"Well, of course, it is better to act on problems before they hurt, while they are still opportunities," said Jack. "But is that kind of proactive leadership possible? Is it possible to get people to take action before their backs are up against the wall?"

"Let us return to England in 1945," Jangbu said. "As soon as the war ended, the citizens of England voted Churchill out of power and said, 'Thank you very much, Winston, for saving the free world, but we don't need you anymore.' However, the economic consequences of the war were far from over. Four years later when England's economy was failing, whom do you suppose they re-elected?"

"Winston Churchill?" asked Jack.

"Exactly," confirmed Jangbu. "Judith M. Bardwick, author of *Danger in the Comfort Zone*, said, 'When conditions are peaceful and the world is relatively certain, people neither need nor want much leadership.'"

"So is it even possible to lead a team to achieve an impossible goal when conditions are peaceful and the world is relatively certain?" Jack asked.

"We shall soon see," said Jangbu.

Leadership by Disruption

"Paul Axtel, a consultant friend of mine, defines leadership as *the ability to disrupt and make it work out,*" explained Jangbu. "In other words, the truly great leaders find a way to create distress and urgency before it is forced upon them from the outside. For political leaders, this is a thankless job. For business leaders, this is the road to huge profits. As an anonymous writer once said, 'For truly great leaders, choice, not chance, determines the destiny of their organization.' For example, in the early 1960s a U.S. President set a big goal. Do you remember what it was?"

"John F. Kennedy set the goal to reach the moon by the end of the decade," Jack said immediately.

"Why did he do it?" asked Jangbu.

"The Soviet Union had just launched Sputnik, and JFK feared that if our space program did not catch up, the U.S.S.R. would be able to launch unopposed nuclear missiles at us from space," said Jack. "He convinced the people of the United States to take action before we were in distress."

"Did people think his goal was impossible?" asked Jangbu.

"Sure they did," said Jack. "My father told me that many people thought the actual moon landing in 1969 was a hoax filmed in the Nevada desert."

Jangbu smiled and nodded.

"So, how do you get people to do the impossible before the emergency hits or when the world around them is relatively stable and secure?" asked Jack.

The Seven Commandments of Breakthrough Leadership

"It is possible," said Jangbu. "You can do it with your teams at work. There are seven commandments you will need to follow."

#1: Learn to have vision

"Confucius said, 'The superior man, while resting in safety, does not forget that danger may come. When in a state of security, he does not forget the possibility of ruin. When all is orderly, he does not forget that disorder may come.'"

"Wow," said Jack. "That makes a lot of sense."

"Vision means seeing a crisis that hasn't happened yet or solving problems that don't hurt yet," Jangbu explained. "Furthermore, it means getting out of the fire-fighting mode. The only way you can do that is by coaching and building your people into teams so they can handle the fires or even prevent them. I do not believe in redefining problems as opportunities. By the time everyone can see them, they really are problems. Opportunities are problems that don't hurt yet, and leaders recognize them before anyone else."

"I see," said Jack. "First you have to see the problems coming and want to do something about them."

#2: Convince the opinion-leaders

"You have a few leaders on your team and many followers," said Jangbu. "Get your leaders committed to the goal by challenging them and making your case to them one on one and then as a group. Your leaders will not need to know exactly how to get to the goal, yet they will understand the need to reach it and will commit to doing it. That is what makes them leaders."

#3: Set a quantitative goal

"Next, you and your leaders will need to set a quantitative goal," continued Jangbu.

"Quantitative?" asked Jack.

"Yes," said Jangbu. "A goal you can measure using numbers. Use some measure of cost, quality or speed. Personally, I think speed is the best choice because the only way to improve speed an impossible amount is to remove non-value-added process steps, which leads simultaneously to improved quality and cost."

#4: Ask your entire team to meet the goal, and keep asking

"This is when it gets really interesting," said Jangbu. "You must ask your entire team as a group to meet the goal and continue to repeat your request."

"But what if some of them don't want to do it?" asked Jack.

"You are not asking them for their permission," said Jangbu. "Simply state your business reasons and your expectation confidently and leave it at that. Tell them that you expect every single person's active support."

#5: Endure the testing

"Gee," said Jack, "it certainly seems like I'd be out on a limb at this point."

"You will be," agreed Jangbu. Many people will pull on your legs and wiggle the tree to try to get you to let go. Why do you think they will do this?"

"I think some people just want to avoid hard work or

change," said Jack. "Others probably feel like they would be hurt by your success."

"You are missing the major reason," said Jangbu.

Jack thought for a moment. Finally he said, "I can't think of any other reasons."

"The main reason your teams will test you is that they want to know if you are committed," said Jangbu.

Jack nodded slowly. "You're right," he said. "Employees in most companies have been disappointed many times by leaders who talked big but gave up quickly."

"They are accustomed to 'programs of the month,' and do not want to commit emotionally to another project only to be let down again by another leader," said Jangbu. "I'll let you in on a secret though. They want you to be for real. So stick to your guns and continue to repeat your expectation. Your leaders will help you behind the scenes, but you've got to be stubborn. You have got to have guts. Your people will resist and resist and resist, but when they finally become convinced that you are committed, they will give in to your will and start to have a lot of fun."

#6: Teach your team creativity

"Once your team has committed to achieving the impossible, they will be ready to think creatively," Jangbu continued. "You will need to study creative techniques and teach them to your team."

"I remember one facilitator who used a great creative technique with us as a management team," Jack said. "He brought a selection of hats to the meeting. Each hat represented a different profession. One person wore a firefighter's hat and thought about how a firefighter would approach the problem. Another wore a cowboy hat, and approached the problem from a cowboy's perspective. The technique really got us out of our habitual ways of thinking."

"Once your team commits to the goal, the only thing standing between them and success is their own ability to discover new solutions," Jangbu said. "There is no truly impossible goal."

#7: Enjoy the ride and the view

"You've told me six commandments," said Jack. "Isn't there one more thing I need to do?"

"Stay out of the way. It is ironic that at this stage, the more you try to help your team develop the solutions, the less motivated they will be," said Jangbu. "The amazing secret is that if you play your role as a leader, you don't need to figure out how to achieve impossible goals. Your team will do it for you. Your reward is seeing them do something they never thought possible. If you want your teams to achieve impossible goals, you have to have the guts to set the goal and stick to it."

CLIMBING TIPS

Before you attempt to lead your team to achieve impossible goals, remember the words of William Ross: *It is fine to aim high if we have developed the ability to accomplish our aims, but there is no use aiming unless our gun is loaded.* So concentrate first on loading your gun. Jack did a lot of work before he was ready to ask his teams to accomplish impossible goals. You will need to build individuals, work cells and teams first.

Lead your team up the mountain to achieve an impossible goal. You will never forget the journey, and your subordinates will thank you forever for bringing them to a pinnacle of such majesty.

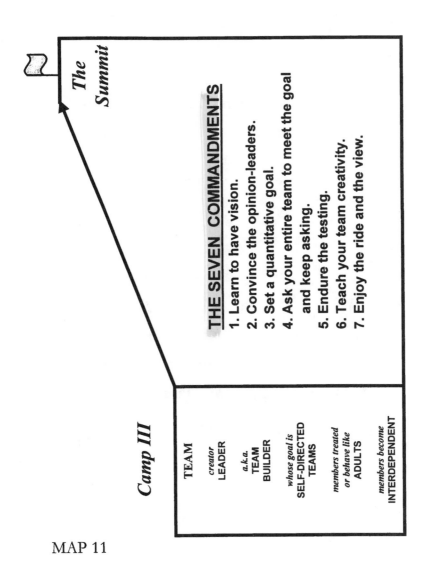

The Summit

THE SEVEN COMMANDMENTS

1. Learn to have vision.
2. Convince the opinion-leaders.
3. Set a quantitative goal.
4. Ask your entire team to meet the goal and keep asking.
5. Endure the testing.
6. Teach your team creativity.
7. Enjoy the ride and the view.

Camp III

TEAM

creator
LEADER

a.k.a.
TEAM
BUILDER

whose goal is
SELF-DIRECTED
TEAMS

members treated
or behave like
ADULTS

members become
INTERDEPENDENT

MAP 11

What I need most is someone to make me do what I can.

- Ralph Waldo Emerson

Your job as a leader is to use the techniques you have learned in this book to make your people do what they can. It is your right and your obligation.

- Jangbu

Results

Marty stood up and banged a fork repeatedly against her empty water glass. In a few moments the room was silent. "A toast," she said as she raised her glass of champagne and looked around the room.

The 32 people in Jack's department were seated at four large tables. Each person had just been served a plate heaped with prime rib, lobster or both.

"I want to officially congratulate you on accomplishing what no one thought you could do," Marty said. "You have cut your lead time from four weeks to two days. When you set that goal six months

189

ago, I have to admit I was doubtful. I didn't want to see you fail so I argued that you should just try for three weeks. Boy, was I wrong."

"Who did you think you were dealing with," yelled Thad, "a bunch of slackers?" Everyone roared with laughter.

"Even I didn't appreciate the talent, energy and creativity you all had inside you," Marty admitted.

"All you had to do was treat us like adults," said Jill from the table to Marty's left. "We always knew how to think like owners instead of employees. You and Jack were smart enough to give us the skills and information we needed to act like owners and patient enough to help us learn."

"I'll never doubt you again," said Marty. She smiled, raised her glass, and they all drank the best champagne they had ever tasted.

Thirty minutes later Jack put his fork down. He was a slow eater. Most of his people had finished eating 10 minutes ago and were scattered around the room talking and laughing. As he leaned back in his chair and wondered if he could still get a cup of coffee, Gary sat down next to him.

"Hey, Gary," Jack greeted him. "I haven't seen you for a couple weeks. How was your vacation?"

"Funny you should ask," Gary said. "I think I'm

losing my mind."

"What are you talking about?" Jack asked.

"Well, after the first week of my vacation," Gary explained, "I told my wife I wanted to go back to work."

"You really are going crazy," Jack said.

"No, Jack, I meant it," Gary said. "You know I've been working hard on helping us get to our lead time goal, right?"

"Sure," said Jack. "I know you came up with many of the ideas that made it possible."

"That's right," said Gary. "But now that we've reached our goal I can't stop thinking of ideas. Every night when I get into bed I get all these ideas in my head, and I can't sleep until I write them down. So I got a pad of paper and put it on my nightstand. I've heard of engineers, scientists and managers doing that, but I never thought I would. I've got my first pad almost full with ideas and diagrams of improvement ideas. I've been dying to go back to work to try them and see if they'll work."

All Jack could do for a moment was smile and nod. Finally he said, "What you just said gives me a greater feeling of satisfaction than anything else we've accomplished as a department."

"It's true, Jack," said Gary, "and everyone else feels the same way. Until we made the Journey To Teams, work had always been the place we had to go to earn enough money to finance the parts of our lives we enjoyed. Now work is enjoyable too. We're working harder than ever, but it's amazing how much fun it is. For years we avoided problems. Getting involved was always such a hassle because management wouldn't listen to us."

"And even when we did listen," Jack interrupted, "we didn't have time to fix the underlying causes. There were simply not enough managers and engineers to solve all the problems and there never will be. We used to think it was our job to make the decisions and solve the problems, but now we know our job is to develop our peoples' ability to do it. Now that you are all able to solve problems and make decisions together, you've not only gotten rid of our old problems, but you've also improved the whole department in hundreds of different ways."

Jack suddenly noticed Jangbu and Marty standing in back of them, listening to their conversation. "The key is challenge," said Jangbu.

"Challenge?" said Jack and Gary together.

"Challenge is what makes life fun and satisfying," Jangbu explained. "It is the reason people climb Everest, and it is the reason Gary now enjoys his work so much."

"I see what you're saying," said Gary. "I've worked for a lot of traditional managers. They took the challenges away from the employees by solving all the problems and making all the decisions for them. Jack gave the challenges back to us and helped us learn to conquer them. At first we thought it was going to be more work for us, but in reality it made our time at work a whole lot more interesting."

"The wonderful thing about capitalism," said Marty, "is that if we choose the right challenges, like you did by improving lead time, we will be rewarded with profits, job security and growth."

"It's been a rewarding Journey," said Jack.

"You've been a great guide, Jangbu," said Marty. "What will you do next?"

"I'm too old for Everest," said Jangbu, "but I will still be a guide. I will help other organizations on their Journey To Teams. That should keep me out of trouble."

Afterward

At the beginning of this book I told you Sir Edmund Hillary became famous for being the first to reach the top of Mount Everest. Did he do it alone? Of course not. There is a group of people who have lived all their lives at the base of the Himalayas. Their bodies have become accustomed to the low levels of oxygen. They know the territory. These people are called Sherpas, and nearly every expedition hires a number of them as guides and equipment carriers.

Sir Edmund Hillary climbed Mount Everest with a Sherpa named Tenzing Norgay. Few people have heard of Norgay, but neither he nor Hillary ever revealed which one of them set foot on the summit first.

At the beginning of each climbing season a group of experienced Sherpas climbs the mountain with long, sharp stakes to pound into the ice and huge coils of brightly colored rope to blaze a trail from bottom to top. They lash ladders as bridges to connect the tops of the huge ice cubes in the Kumbu Icefall to make the climbing faster and safer. Many experienced climbers complain that climbing the mountain has become like a carnival ride, requiring little skill. That is an exaggeration, but with the help of experienced Sherpas, many amateur climbers have succeeded where only the best climbers succeeded in the past. Everest Consulting Group may be able to help you on your journey as well. Our contact information is below, and we'd be delighted to hear from you.

* * *

EXPERIENCED SHERPAS FOR HIRE

Don't get lost on your Journey To Teams. We've got the route marked.

Invite Michael Regan and his experienced staff to help you on your Journey To Teams. Whether you are looking for **comprehensive training and consulting** assistance or a **keynote speech** at your next meeting, we can help.

Call 1-888-910-8326 for more information.

www.everestcg.com

Books for Coaches

"Jangbu," said Marty, "I would like one of my staff members to become an expert on teams. I think the best person would be my training manager. Can you recommend what training he should get so that my managers and supervisors can go to him when they have a question during our Journey To Teams?"

Marty and Jangbu were having a late lunch one afternoon. Jack was on vacation. Jangbu thought about Marty's question for a moment before answering.

"Why not have your managers and supervisors become experts in teams?" Jangbu asked. "In order to be good coaches and leaders they will have to have the concepts firmly planted in their brains. If they have to depend on someone else to give them the answers, they probably won't know enough to be effective anyway."

"That would be great, but I can't afford to send them all to training," she explained. "That's why I wanted to concentrate on getting one person really educated."

"Training classes are not the only way to learn," Jangbu replied. "Certainly they should be part of the learning mix, but they should not be the primary ingredient. I learned almost everything I know about teams from two sources: experience on Mount Everest and good books. Your managers are already getting the experience. Why not get them to read the books?"

Marty frowned. "The majority of my managers and supervisors probably couldn't tell you the last time they read a business book," she said. "I'm not sure I would feel comfortable giving them books to read at home. I don't think many of them would do it."

"Who said anything about reading at home?" Jangbu asked. "If your managers and supervisors are acting as coaches they should be recovering a lot of the time they previously spent fighting fires on the shop floor. I suggest that you remind them of that and tell them that part of being a leader is taking responsibility for their own growth and education. So give them the books and ask them to read for at least an hour each day at work. Tell them you are paying them to learn and it is now part of their job expectations. As a matter of fact, once you have implemented real teams, your supervisors should be spending a minimum of 10 hours a week doing nothing but reading and learning. Managers, on the other hand, should spend at least 20 hours a week reading and learning. They will be teaching their subordinates to make even bigger and more complex decisions, decisions that even they as managers and supervisors are not prepared to make on their own today."

Marty leaned back in her chair. "Wow," she said. "I guess that makes sense. Maybe we could all read the same book at the same time. Our goal could be a certain number of chapters each week. Once a week we could get together and discuss how the ideas in the books apply to us. Can you suggest any books for us to read?"

"As a matter of fact, I can," Jangbu replied. "I'll write them down for you. I suggest buying a copy of each book for each of your supervisors and managers. Encourage them to read actively by underlining or highlighting the parts they like and writing their opinions and questions in the margins. It will increase retention noticeably."

Jangbu's Recommendations*:

1. *The Journey To Teams: The New Approach to Breakthrough Business Performance*, by Michael D. Regan.

2. *Managing Transitions: Making the Most of Change*, by William Bridges.

3. *Discipline Without Punishment*, by Richard Grote.

4. *Zapp!: The Lightning of Empowerment: How to Improve Quality, Productivity, and Employee Satisfaction*, by William C. Byham, Ph.D. and Jeff Cox.

5. *Maverick: The Success Story Behind the World's Most Unusual Workplace*, by Ricardo Semler.

6. *Peopleware: Productive Projects and Teams*, by Tom Demarco and Timothy Lister.

7. *The Kaizen Revolution: How to Use Kaizen Events to Double Your Profits*, by Michael D. Regan.

---

* Everest Consulting Group stocks these books for your convenience. We will deliver them to you at list price plus shipping on request. Call us toll free at 1-888-910-8326.

The Kaizen Revolution

The following is an excerpt from *The Kaizen Revolution: How to Use Kaizen Events to Double Your Profits*, by Michael D. Regan.

*   *   *

Bite off more than you can chew, then chew it. Plan more than you can do, then do it.   - Anonymous

Note From the Author

What are Kaizen Events, and can you really use them to double your profits? A Kaizen Event is a focused, week-long improvement effort. A well-planned and expertly led event can produce one or more of the following results: lead time and work-in-process reduced by 80 percent, scrap reduced by 50 percent, and productivity increased by 30 percent. These improvements will help you simultaneously increase your market share and reduce your costs, resulting in dramatically better profits.

The ideas in this book are presented in the form of a story for ease of reading and maximum learning. Each chapter ends with a summary of key points for efficient review.

Dive into this book, dream about what you can accomplish, and then go out and do it.

Michael D. Regan

Raleigh, NC

February 2000

Sample chapter from
The Kaizen Revolution

Kaizen Event Preparation

Monday, April 19   5:40 a.m.   Conference Room

"Let's start by reviewing our overall lean manufacturing implementation strategy," Roger said. "Here are the steps:

1. Teach everyone 5S and start implementing it everywhere in the plant.
2. Choose a product for a model line, to serve as an example or pattern for the rest of our

202

products.

3. Implement work cells, continuous one-piece flow, and standard work in final assembly.

4. Build work cells in component fabrication and use kanban to connect them to final assembly. Reduce setup time and batch sizes and implement preventive maintenance.

5. Apply everything we learned on our first model product line to all of our other products.

"We established our overall goals of 90 percent lead time reduction, 5,000 defects per million products produced, and 20 percent productivity improvements for the next two years," Roger said. "I'm leading the third of 10 scheduled 5S implementation sessions starting at 7:00 a.m., which is why we are meeting so early today. As you all have heard, Evanson made a big wind-up alarm clock sale for us, so that is where we'll focus."

"Great," said Sam. "So we'll use a Kaizen Event to implement work cells, continuous one-piece flow, and standard work in final assembly, right?"

"Right," said Roger.

"How do we start?" asked Kim.

"With preparation," said Roger. "Preparation is critical for a successful Kaizen Event. The first thing we need to do is define the scope of the Kaizen Event. Where does this event start and where does it end?"

"I would say it starts when all the component parts have been delivered to assembly, and ends when the product is packaged and ready for delivery to finished goods inventory," said Kim.

"Good," said Roger. "Next we must choose a team leader for the Kaizen Event. We need a person from outside the area we are improving so that he or she will bring fresh thinking to our improvement efforts. The leader also must know how to be a coach, how to get other people to think of improvements and implement them. We also need to choose a leader-in-training for this event for two reasons: first, we need more leaders to run more events, and second, the leader often needs help coordinating all the activities during an event. I will be the first team leader. Our first leader-in-training will be Tom."

"But I don't have the experience, and I don't understand this stuff very well," Tom said.

"You'll learn," said Roger. "Lean manufacturing is the strategy we're using to turn this company around, and you must understand and actively lead this effort with me*."

Tom shrugged and nodded weakly.

"Next," continued Roger, "the team leaders must study and understand the process in order to determine achievable breakthrough goals for the event in terms of quality, cost, and delivery. By applying my lean manufacturing experience to a process, I can usually picture how to improve lead time by up to 90 percent, productivity up to 50 percent, and quality up to 75 percent. Those are breakthrough goals, but they are achievable. You will develop the same kind of judgment after you've been through a number of Kaizen Events."

"How do you study an area?" asked Kim.

"I make products," said Roger. "I like to start at the beginning and have the operators teach me each operation. Then I have them watch me do it. Doing the job yourself is the only way to learn the details. Of course, I also look at the levels of inventory, the way the

---

* Joseph C. Day, CEO of Freudenberg-NOK, spent 35 percent of his time working with Kaizen teams during the first two years of lean manufacturing implementation. As a result, his company increased sales in four years from $200 million to $600 million with record profits. They have held 2,500 kaizen events in 15 manufacturing plants and involved 90 percent of their 3,500 associates. From *Becoming Lean*, by Jeffrey K. Liker.

equipment and tables are arranged, the volume of product, the causes of defects, and the attitudes and skills of the people in the area. I don't have a 5S implementation session tomorrow, so Tom and I will spend the entire day learning about the area. We'll meet again as a management team tomorrow afternoon to discuss the goals."

*   *   *

Tuesday, April 20   4:45 p.m.   Conference Room

"Roger and I made lots of products today," said Tom, "and we studied the wind-up alarm clock assembly area. Based on Roger's lean manufacturing experience, we think the following goals are achievable:

- Reduce work-in-process inventory by 80 percent
- Reduce lead time (from fabricated parts to packaged product) by 90 percent
- Reduce defects by 50 percent
- Improve productivity by 30 percent

"We can accomplish these goals by implementing work cells, continuous one-piece flow, and standard work," Tom concluded.

"Good goals," said Roger. "Next we need to choose a week for the event. I suggest we start on Monday, April 26, which will give us time to finish our preparations."

"In the next few days," he continued, "we will need to meet with all the employees in the area to explain the Kaizen Event goals, what we will be doing during the kaizen week, and ask for their ideas for improvement."

"I like that idea," said Maria. "We'll collect their ideas and give them to the Kaizen team to implement. That way, the people not on the Kaizen team will have more buy-in to the changes in their area."

"Next, we will need to choose the Kaizen team members," said Roger. "We've already got our team leader and team leader-in-training. A Kaizen team should have eight to 15 members, and approximately 70 percent of them should be non-managers and people from the shop floor."

"Why?" asked Maria.

"Because we want to use Kaizen Events as a way to give our shop floor folks a chance to make changes," said Roger. "When you get too many salaried people together they talk too much and the hourly employees get discouraged and stop participating. There are a lot more brains on the shop floor than in the front office, and we need to tap into them. The salaried people on the Kaizen team will be coaches, not thinkers and implementers."

"That makes sense," said Maria.

"Let's start by assuming our first event will have 12 people," said Roger. "Counting Tom and me, we have room for at most two more salaried team members, and they should come from the management team to get you involved early. As salaried team members, I will expect you to serve as coaches to keep the sub-teams on track during the event, in addition to providing ideas and enthusiasm."

"I'd love to volunteer, but I'm too busy defending us against our creditors," said Maria.

"I understand," said Roger. "Sam, you should be one of the team members."

"Great," said Sam.

"Paul," said Roger, "as quality manager you should be on this team. The work cells will be taking responsibility for their own quality control."

"I don't think I'd be of much help," said Paul, his arms crossed in front of him. "I don't agree with this lean stuff. I haven't from the start, and you haven't listened to my objections."

Roger stared at him and paused. "You made a commitment to help us implement lean manufacturing when you signed the paper in my office. In order for you to stay with this company, you will need to suppress your disagreement from this moment forward and commit yourself to supporting this effort with every word you speak and action you take," Roger finally said. "Will you do that?"

"I have a right to my opinion," Paul snapped back.

"The decision to implement lean manufacturing at this plant was made when you hired me," said Roger. "I will tolerate no opposition to that decision from any employee of this company."

"I didn't vote to hire you," Paul responded. "And that's not a very nice way to talk."

"Nice isn't my goal."

"I thought you were supposed to be a big 'team' guy," said Paul. "People on teams are supposed to be nice to each other."

"People on teams are supposed to share a common

goal," said Roger. "If you don't share our goal of implementing lean manufacturing, you can't be on the team."

Paul stood up. "These lean ideas will sink this company," he said. "And Roy feels the same way."

Roy turned to look at Paul, clearly angry, but silent.

"Will everyone but Paul please leave the room?" Roger asked.

They all rose and silently left the room. Roger closed the door behind them.

"Paul," said Roger, "you're fired."

"I figured that."

*   *   *

"Paul has chosen to leave the company," announced Roger. "Roy, as engineering manager, you would be an excellent choice for our last salaried spot on the Kaizen team."

"As Paul said," Roy responded, "I'm not completely comfortable with lean manufacturing. It's the opposite of what I've believed for 30 years. But I'm willing to swallow my disagreement and do my best to help."

"That's all I ask," said Roger. "We need to fill the

remaining eight slots with non-managers and people from the shop floor. It is often important to ensure maintenance support for a Kaizen Event, and because we will be moving equipment and electrical drops, we should have a maintenance technician as a team member. It is also helpful to involve a supplier or customer on the team, so we will invite one or the other for this event."

"I know a buyer I'd like to invite," said Evanson. "I told him what we're doing to improve, and he'd be interested in participating."

"Invite him," said Roger. "We have six spots left and they should all go to shop floor employees."

"Should we ask for volunteers?" asked Kim.

"No," said Roger. "Not for the first Kaizen Event. In every department in a plant, there are those hourly employees who influence their peers. Their opinions tend to become the opinions of most everyone else. We will identify the 'opinion-leaders' and ask them to be on the team. A properly managed Kaizen Event is a wonderful experience for most hourly employees, and we want people who will spread the word for us. We'll choose four people from wind-up assembly and two people from the departments that fabricate parts for them."

"I know who most of the opinion-leaders are," said Kim.

"Me too," said Sam.

"I suggest you two put a list together," said Roger, "and run it by Roy too. Then we'll ask them to join the team. You must understand that team members are dedicated to the Kaizen team for the entire week. Get someone to handle your regular job for the week, get rid of your pager, and tell everyone else to pretend you're on vacation."

"I assume that alarm clock production will be interrupted for part of the week," noted Kim. "I'll look at our inventory and ensure that we build enough product before the event to enable a week-long shut down."

"There will be some disruption to the schedule as we move equipment and experiment with different layouts," said Roger. "Plan on half the normal production from that area. In addition, I would like you to take on the role of acting manufacturing manager in addition to your duties in production control. Can you handle it?"

"I'll do it," said Kim.

"Roger," said Roy, "you believe we will get an immediate productivity improvement from this first event, right?"

"Yes," said Roger, "at least 20 percent."

"There are 30 people assigned to wind-up assembly," continued Roy. "Let's say during the event we reduce that by six. You promised no more layoffs, so do you have a plan to reassign employees freed up due to productivity improvements?"

"Eventually," explained Roger, "they will be needed for production because we are going to grow, right Evanson?"

"Sure boss," said Evanson. "If you give me better quality, cost and delivery, I can sell as many clocks as you make."

"Once they've had time to cross train," continued Roger, "I will take the best six people out of wind-up assembly and assign them to our brand new 'Kaizen department', reporting directly to me. They will work on improvement projects throughout the plant."

"Is there anything else we need to do to prepare for our first Kaizen Event?" asked Roy.

"Just a few more details," said Roger. "We need to have a carpenter available to build new tables and storage racks during the event."

"I know the perfect person," said Roy. "She's a quick

worker."

"Fine," said Roger. "Make sure she's available. We also need to identify administrative support for the team. We'll use Tom's executive assistant, since he has nothing for her to do yet. She will order t-shirts and plaques as recognition for the team members, arrange for lunch to be brought in each day, reserve a conference room near the shop floor for training and discussion, and make sure we have supplies: flip charts, markers, pens, pencils, scratch paper, stopwatches, rulers, calculators, tape, scissors, tables and chairs for everyone, notebook computer, LCD projector, video camera with tripod, blank tapes, television and VCR, name tags, clipboards, masking tape, sticky notes, and tape measure."

"Sounds like you've done a few of these Kaizen Events," said Tom. "Anything else we need to do?"

"Two more things," said Roger. "We need to get approval for overtime to be used during the week as necessary. If we manage the event correctly, we won't need much of it. I hereby approve the overtime. Finally, dress casually for the event. You will be working on the shop floor and getting dirty. No suits or ties."

"How often will we do Kaizen Events?" asked Roy.

"Given the circumstances, we need to plan on doing

another event as soon as this one is finished, and we'll start planning that one right now," said Roger. "Tom, you'll be the leader of the next event. It will be your responsibility to plan it. I will coach you."

"Where is this next event going to be?" asked Tom.

"Work with Kim and figure out which fabricated wind-up alarm clock component has the most quality problems and the longest lead time," said Roger. "That's the one on which we'll focus."

CHAPTER SUMMARY

Pre-Event Preparation Checklist

✓ Define the scope

✓ Choose a team leader

✓ Choose a team leader-in-training

✓ Study the process and determine achievable breakthrough goals

✓ Choose a week for the event

✓ Meet with all the employees in the area to explain the Kaizen Event goals, explain what the team will be doing during the Kaizen week, and ask for their improvement ideas

✓ Choose eight to 15 members. About 70 percent of them should be non-managers and people from the shop floor

✓ Ensure maintenance support

✓ Involve a supplier and/or a customer

✓ Identify the "opinion-leaders" and ask them to be on the team

✓ Ensure that team members are dedicated to the Kaizen team for the entire week

✓ Build product before the event to enable a week-long shut down

✓ Plan to reassign employees freed up due to productivity improvements

✓ Have a carpenter available to build new tables and storage units

✓ Identify administrative support for the team

✓ Order t-shirts and plaques as recognition for the team members

✓ Arrange for lunch to be brought in each day

✓ Reserve a conference room near the shop floor for training and discussion

✓ Get approval for overtime

✓ Dress casually for the event

✓ Gather supplies: flip charts, markers, calculators, tables and chairs, notebook computer, LCD projector, video camera with tripod, blank tapes, television and VCR, clipboards, sticky notes, etc.

*　　*　　*

Call 1-888-910-8326 to order your copy of
The Kaizen Revolution

Three bonus articles by
Michael D. Regan

THE BIGGEST BARRIER TO TEAMS:
TRADITIONAL SUPERVISORS

No matter what kind of training you give your individual contributors, if you still have traditional supervisors, your efforts to implement teams will fail. Why? Here's how a traditional teambuilding program usually works (see if this sounds familiar): send all your individual contributors to a series of full-day training classes on topics like communication, problem solving, and conflict resolution. Throw in some personality testing for good measure. Then change some labels: start referring to departments as "teams", and supervisors as "coaches." You're done! Now you just sit back and wait for the results.

Nice theory. Unfortunately, it never works. Why? You've told your individual contributors that you want them to start taking responsibility for solving problems and making decisions. They're fired up - ready to change the world.

However, your traditional supervisors got promoted or hired because they had proven their ability to solve problems and make decisions. They've been doing it (just like their managers told them to) for years, even decades. What do you think is going to happen the first time a decision of any significance has to be made? Or the first time any real problem is discovered? You know the answer - the traditional supervisor is going to take over. He's never trusted his people with anything important, and he's not going to start now.

How do the individual contributors on the "team" react to this? You're right again - they think this whole "teaming" thing is a bunch of bologna, another worthless, time-wasting "program of the month." Morale sinks again, and "teaming" is over. The most pathetic part is that management doesn't even realize it. They keep bumbling along talking about teams and pathetic part is that management doesn't even realize it. They keep bumbling along talking about teams and teamwork, but the organization hasn't changed a bit, except perhaps that everyone has even less faith in management than they did before this latest misadventure.

The biggest barrier to real teams is traditional supervisors, because their job is to solve problems and make decisions. Until they learn to stop doing that, and start coaching their individual contributors to solve problems and make decisions, you are dead in the water. You need professional coaches. To learn more, call us at 1-888-910-8326.

*   *   *

Sales Hall of Fame

"Hey Rod, don't forget we've got our first CAX Coaches meeting after work today," Tim said as he was passing Rod's open office door.

"Oh yeah, I can't think of a better way to waste two hours," Rod shot back. Looking out his office door he asked his administrative assistant, "Cindy, can you please let Mike know when he calls in that the Eber quote is in his mail box and he can pick it up whenever he gets in? Thanks." Rod was picking up his notebook and grabbing a pen on the way out of his office when Caroline appeared at the door.

Caroline said, "I hope you weren't planning on going anywhere for the next hour or so. You were the one who said this proposal had to get out today and you've already told me to come back twice earlier today."

"I'm sorry but I've to go to this mandatory managers meeting and I'm running late already. I'll catch up to you tomorrow morning. OK?" Rod asked.

"Well, don't say a word to me if we lose the Hastings deal because we're late with our proposal. You did the same thing to me when it came time for our presentation. Aren't we supposed to be selling here? All I do is wait around until you've the time to meet with me. I've got better things to do," she said and stormed off.

"Another satisfied customer. I'll deal with her later. I've got to go now. She's right though. Instead of having to attend a useless meeting I should be selling," Rod said to himself as he started to jog towards the cafeteria for the meeting.

*   *   *

"Can you give us some hard examples of how we might use coaching in managing a sales region?" someone from the audience was asking just as Rod walked in.

"Sure, I'm certain that's a question on all of your minds," Gary, the instructor, responded.

"I've never been asked about my team building expertise at the end of a quarter," an anonymous manager volunteered. Several in the audience were laughing at that comment.

"Let's try something that might help clarify the point. How many sports fans in the audience? Show of hands, please?" Gary asked. Just about every one raised their hand. "Okay, first, choose a sport that requires a coach. Then take a minute and write the names of those who have been elected to that sports Hall of Fame as a coach and a player." He let a few minutes pass and asked, "Anyone have one?" There was nothing but silence. Gary finally said, "There are only eight that I could find in all of sports- two in basketball and six in football. Doesn't it seem strange that from all the hundreds of Hall of Fame inductees in sports that less than one percent excelled at both playing and coaching? How can you explain this?" More silence. Gary went on, "A large part of the answer is that being a great coach is a completely different skill set than being a great individual player. If it was the same skill, finding great coaches would be easy and they wouldn't get fired every year." He continued, "The same is true in selling. I suspect most of you're still behaving like great sales people but not great coaches. A sure sign of this is if your staff is following you around waiting for you to tell them what to do, how to do it and when. They'll wait for hours until you give them the answer and worst of all, you'll let them waste their time waiting. Anybody see themselves in this description?" Gary asked.

"That can't be me, can it?" Rod thought to himself, feeling somewhat embarrassed. Down deep he knew Gary's last statement was the truth.

"Sales Managers need to coach their people to be the best they can be. You do that by teaching them how to think and solve problems without you. The fact that they can't do this today is why you need to become a great coach today. This course requires your commitment to stop being a roadblock to their success and to make a full commitment to becoming a great

223

coach. Agreed?" Everyone in the room nodded. "Let's get started." Gary said.

*   *   *

Rod came into the office the next morning and went straight to Caroline's cubicle and said "Good morning, Caroline. I've got some good news and some great news. First, as a result of what I learned yesterday I'm no longer in the proposal writing and presentation business. Second, you and the others are now going to write your own proposals, quotes and presentations. I'll be here to coach you and give you the benefit of my experience but as of now it's your job," he told her.

"Where is the good news in that? I don't think anyone in this sales region has ever done any one of those things by themselves. Do you have any idea how long that's going to take me to do it myself? Give me a break," Caroline shot back rolling her eyes.

"Hold on. Yesterday you gave me a hard time because I wasn't there when you wanted me to write the proposal and now that I'm stepping aside and letting you take control of the process, I'm still getting grief? If what you wanted all along was your own personal proposal writer, then that was never my job to begin with. It's your job to think through and respond to whatever needs to be done to meet the client's needs. My job, as coach, is to assist and help you become the best you can be. I'm committed to doing just that," he said.

"You honestly think this is going to be better for the client than what we've been doing? Based on my lack of experience in doing this kind of stuff, it's going to take forever to get things out to a client," Caroline declared.

"Initially it will probably take some time but I'm certain you'll master it quickly. Before long writing proposals, creating presentations and most importantly winning more business on your own will become second nature. I'll be there to assist you in anyway possible but I won't do it for you anymore," Rod said.

"Oh, I see. Well, if that's the way it's going to be I need to get going. How do I even get started?" she asked.

"Well, first things first. What are you trying to tell Hastings in the proposal?" Rod asked.

"To tell them why they should select CAX as their supplier?" Caroline asked.

"That's a start. Do you believe they should select us?" he asked.

"Definitely!" she replied.

"Why?" he asked.

"Our single product will eliminate their reliance on the two suppliers they use today. They have to assemble the parts they get from them to do the same thing we can provide in a single component out of the box with no assembly. The assembly process has led to quality issues and then coordinating deliveries between the two suppliers has slowed their responsiveness to customers. All around we're a great fit for them." Caroline exclaimed.

"Whoa, slow down. We have to make sure we get all these down. What do you think you should do with all these great reasons?" Rod asked.

"I guess I should list them to make certain I've got them all, and then maybe put them in their order of importance to Hastings?" she asked.

"You're on the right track. Then what's next?" he asked.

"Write an outline for the proposal?" Caroline asked.

"Right. Does your list help you with the outline in any way?" Rod asked.

"The outline and the proposal should definitely follow the order of importance for selecting CAX so the strongest reasons are stated up front. Then once I make the business case the pricing information should follow, I guess," she said.

"Ok. Then what?" Rod asked.

"Write a draft proposal?" Caroline asked.

"I love it when a plan comes together. See you can do this by yourself. Once you've got a draft ready come by my office, and we'll go over it together and make certain you've covered all the points. We should be able to send it to Hastings today." he said.

"Well, that sounds good but I better get started on this if I've got to get it finished today. I'll plan on having a draft for you by 2PM, is that alright?" she asked.

"Sounds great, just come by my office when you're ready. I'm certain you'll do just fine. See you later," Rod said and left. He went to talk to the other sales people to give them the good news. "I wonder if CAX even has a Hall of Fame," Rod thought to himself as he walked down the hallway.

Additional Resources

- Everest Consulting Group can help you transform your managers and supervisors into effective coaches. We also deliver comprehensive training, consulting and keynote speeches in the areas of leadership, kaizen, and lean manufacturing. Call toll free 1-888-910-8326 to learn more.

- To subscribe to our TEAM ANSWERS or our KAIZEN / LEAN MANUFACTURING e-mail newsletter, visit www.everestcg.com.

- Explore our web site at www.everestcg.com.